A PERSONAL NARRATIVE

OF

THIRTEEN YEARS SERVICE

AMONGST THE

WILD TRIBES OF KHONDISTAN

FOR THE

SUPPRESSION OF HUMAN SACRIFICE

A PERSONAL NARRATIVE

OF

THIRTEEN YEARS SERVICE

AMONGST THE

WILD TRIBES OF KHONDISTAN

FOR THE

SUPPRESSION OF HUMAN SACRIFICE.

BY

MAJOR GENERAL JOHN CAMPBELL, C.B.

GYAN

Published by

GYAN

Gyan Publishing House
5, Ansari Road
Daryaganj, New Delhi-110002
Phone: 011-47034999, 9811692060
E-mail: books@gyanbooks.com

Distribution Network
gyanbooks.com
India, USA, Canada, UK, Australia

ISBN: 978-93-6208-294-7 (HB)
First Published, 1864

2nd Impression 2024

Printed at: Gyan Press, Delhi.

A PERSONAL NARRATIVE OF THIRTEEN YEARS SERVICE AMONGST THE WILD TRIBES OF KHONDISTAN FOR THE SUPPRESSION OF HUMAN SACRIFICE
Author: MAJOR GENERAL JOHN CAMPBELL

A PERSONAL NARRATIVE

OF

THIRTEEN YEARS SERVICE

AMONGST THE

WILD TRIBES OF KHONDISTAN

FOR THE

SUPPRESSION OF HUMAN SACRIFICE.

BY

MAJOR GENERAL JOHN CAMPBELL, C. B.

LONDON:
HURST AND BLACKETT, PUBLISHERS,
SUCCESSORS TO HENRY COLBURN,
13, GREAT MARLBOROUGH STREET.
1864.

CONTENTS.

CHAPTER III.

CHAPTER IV.

CHAPTER V.

CHAPTER VI.

CHAPTER VII.

CHAPTER VIII.

CHAPTER IX.

CHAPTER X.

CHAPTER XI.

CHAPTER XII.

CHAPTER XIII.

CHAPTER XIV.

CHAPTER XV.

CHAPTER XVI.

ILLUSTRATIONS.

For a more particular description of the above Illustrations, see Appendix, p. 316.

CHAPTER I.

GEOGRAPHY OF ORISSA—CHANGES OF MASTERS—ITS CONDITION AS A PORTION OF BRITISH INDIA—ANTIQUITIES IN THE ANCIENT CAPITAL—NOVELTY IN AGRICULTURE—REMAINS OF NATIVE SCULPTURE IN THE TEMPLE OF GRAMESWARA—TRAVELS OF A CHINESE HIOCIEN THSANG—HIS ACCOUNT OF THE CAPITAL—RUINED CITY OF BHUHANESAR—ROCK CAVES OF KHANDIGIRI—TEMPLE OF THE SUN AT KANARAK—MILITARY OPERATIONS OF THE EAST INDIA COMPANY IN ORISSA AT THE COMMENCEMENT OF THE PRESENT CENTURY—WILD TRIBES OF THE HILL DISTRICTS—VEGETATION—VILLAGES—THE KHONDS—CULTIVATION OF COTTON—COSTUME AND ARMS—MUSIC—DRESS—FOOD—COURT CEREMONIALS—OORYA AND KHOND LANGUAGES—PROCEEDINGS OF THE MISSIONARIES IN KHONDISTAN.

CHAPTER I.

It is probable that in England few persons possess any great knowledge of that portion of our Indian empire which is formed out of the kingdom of Orissa, and still fewer take any interest in its ancient or modern history. Although this narrative will have almost exclusive reference to the Khonds and tribes inhabiting the mountain ranges of this once renowned sovereignty, it may not be unacceptable to general readers to learn some particulars of a province once held in the highest estimation in the East.

Orissa lies between the eighteenth and twenty-third parallels of north latitude, and the eighty-third and eighty-seventh of east longitude. Its boundaries are the Bay of Bengal on the east, Gondwana on the west, the river Godavery on the south, and Behar and Bengal on the north. Its extreme length is about four hundred miles, its average breadth seventy; and it encloses an area of twenty-eight thousand square miles. This description, however, it must be observed, applies to the low country as well as to the hills, but the tribes amongst whom I so long laboured inhabit the latter only, and deserve to be regarded as amongst the most interesting vestiges of the ancient kingdom.

A great Oriental scholar has said, that "of all the regions of the earth, Burata Khond is the most distinguished; and of all the regions of Burata Khond, Utkala Khond boasts the highest renown. In its entire extent it is a place of pious pilgrimage. Its happy inhabitants live secure of a reception into the world of spirits, and those who visit the country, and bathe in its sacred rivers, obtain remission of their sins, though they may be as heavy as mountains. Who shall adequately describe its blessed streams," continues the enthusiastic Pundit, "its holy temples, its fragrant flowers, its delicious fruits, and all the attractions and advantages of dwelling in so favoured a land? But where can be the necessity of attempting its panegyric?—it is a paradise, in which the devotees delight to dwell."

Bharadwagee Muni, in the Russila Sanhita, another Indian authority, one of the famous generals of the renowned Emperor Akbar, when marching an army through this attractive province, was so amazed at the crowd of Brahmins who peopled it, the magnificent stone temples and other structures of its ancient capital, Bhuvaneswar, and by the marvellous beauty of the holy river, Mahanuddy, that flowed through its verdant lands, that he solemnly exclaimed, "It is not proper that this country should be sought as an object of human ambition, it belongs exclusively to the Gods; it is a place of continual pilgrimage."

The country once so highly esteemed appears to have parted with the majority of its claims to such regard, for the English traveller might penetrate its jungles and its marshes, climb its steepest hills and ford its deepest rivers, without coming upon any evidence either of the wonderful beauty of its landscape, or the marvellous magnificence of its cities.

Orissa has had several changes of masters. An inscription found on a stone taken from a temple in Cuttack, translated in the Journal of the Asiatic Society of Bengal, commences with reference to its conquest, by Janamajaya, the King of Telinga; but the country had been appropriated by foreign conquerors long before. India suffered under three moral cataclasms, that produced the most complete revolution; these were the Buddhistic, the Brahminical, and the Mahomedan, and their influence penetrated to Orissa. Some remains of its ancient greatness were evident as late as the year 1838, when

Lieutenant Kittoe, during a tour in the country, acknowledged that it possessed more temples, sacred spots, and relics, than any other province in Hindostan.

The ancient Orissa, as it existed under the rule of the Princes of the Gunga Vansa line for nearly four centuries as an independent monarchy, or as it flourished as a principality of the Mogul empire, is scarcely to be recognised in that dependency of British India, now known as the Zillah of Cuttack, which includes the most considerable portion of the hill districts or country of the Khonds. It has gone on diminishing in extent from the conquests of the Uria or Ooryah nation (whence its name), when it included a considerable portion of Bengal and Telingana, till it was confined to what was known more than fifty years ago as the district of Cuttack, to which Mr. Sterling devoted a quarto volume, entitled, "An Account, Geographical, Statistical, and Historical of Orissa Proper, or Cuttack."

Much of the country, which native authorities describe as the Eden of their deities, is in a state of wilderness, marshy woodland and thick forest, abounding in wild animals; and the enterprising English sportsmen, who have penetrated these haunts of the tiger, the panther, the buffalo, and the bear, have brought back, with the spoils of the chase, only slight contributions towards a knowledge of the geography of the district. As a sketch of the natural history of the country will be found in the concluding chapter of this volume, I shall confine my attention here to an account of some interesting features of its history.

Lieutenant Kittoe made an exploration of the country in the year 1838, an account of which he published in the Journal of the Asiatic Society of Bengal of that year. Of the ancient capital of the kingdom, which he calls Kurda, at the time of his visit, nothing remained but the rough walls of the palace, and some of the gateways of the city. He describes the temples on the hill of Kassilás, a place of pilgrimage, as well as an annual fair for the people of Orissa, and other ancient temples at Badèswar. At Atturva, a considerable village on the banks of the Brahmini, he met for the first time with large herds of buffaloes and other cattle, and came upon an extensive field of cultivation.

"I here," he states, "observed a method of tilling the land quite novel to me; the fields are dug with long and heavy crow-bars, each clod, as it is turned up, is bruised with the bar, and thus prepared for the seed without using the plough; indeed, the stiff nature of the soil would not admit of its being ploughed in the dry season. This practice I found to prevail throughout the valley of the Brahmini, which tract is very fertile."

His description of the sculptures in the temple of Grameswara, near Ratrapan, shows to what extent the art had been cultivated in Orissa in the era of its prosperity, and his transcripts of the various inscriptions discovered by him at Dhauli, in Cuttack, discovered to be edicts promulgated by Asoka, king of India, assist in establishing the ancient importance of the country.

A few historical notices may be gleaned from much earlier authorities, and I will refer to some of them in illustration of the bygone greatness of Orissa.

A Chinese traveller, disguised as a religious mendicant, penetrated this now obscure district within the second quarter of the seventh century, when it was a place thought worthy of being visited by a great man on his travels. This personage, who was known as Hiocien Thsang, managed to achieve a durable reputation for himself among his countrymen for his geographical knowledge. His travels in India were compiled by two of his scholars, and have been translated into French by M. Stanislas Julien.*

There is another work,† produced in the Central

* Histoire de la Vie de Hiocien Thsang, et de ses Voyages dans l'Inde, depuis l'an 629 jusq'en 645.

† "Si-ya-ki, ou Mémoires sur les Contrées Occidentales."

Flowery Land, by a distinguished Chinese author, known as Pien-ki, which M. Julien has also translated. It describes the adventures of the illustrious Hiocien Thsang. From both these works a digest has been made for English oriental scholars by the late Professor H. H. Wilson, for the Royal Asiatic Society of Great Britain, and is published in the thirteenth volume of their Journal.

From this account it is evident that, before the middle of the seventh century, the capital of the kingdom of U-cha (Orissa), where Hiocien Thsang remained for some time, was an important city, and the seat of a powerful government. Indian reports, therefore, of the glorious past of this land of jungle and barbarism, are not to be entirely discredited. The narrative is very curious—indeed, the picture it gives of Hindostan and the adjoining countries, during the sixteen years' wanderings of the accomplished traveller, deserves to be regarded as unique. He anticipated Marco Polo by about six hundred years, and explored a much larger portion of India. So complete, however, are the changes which have passed over nearly all these states since his visit, that it is very difficult to identify the places he describes. There is room for very little question, however, that the people of Orissa, at this date, were better off than their contemporary Anglo-Saxons.

Among the monuments of interest in Orissa is the ruined city Bhuhanesan. A recent explorer says:—"The traveller emerges all at once from paddy fields into the midst of a deserted city—another Palmyra—ruins of temples all around, but no worshippers." * These are vestiges of a greatness that has long passed away. Similar changes have fallen upon African cities, but in India they are not confined to this district. Jungle may have overgrown many of its popular places, just as a similar rank vegetation has obliterated the residence of the once powerful Janak and his court, in the Nepal Terai—five such cities and a busy population have been swept away from the Sunderbunds, and the ruins of another are to be found in Perulia.

About six miles from the Palmyra, are to be found the rock-cut caves of Khandigiri, where a colony of Buddhist hermit monks once resided, their Pali inscriptions having stood there for at least two thousand years. One of the verandahs has been fashioned like a tiger's head, yet probably that animal was less a subject of superstitious regard to the ancient Orissans than it is to their descendants, the increase in the jungle having made its savage characteristics more familiar to and more dreaded by the latter.

* Rev. J. Long. "Notes and Queries suggested by a Visit to Orissa, in 1859." Journal of Asiatic Sociey of Bengal, xxxiii., 194.

The temple of the sun at Kanárak, erected about the twelfth century, is ornamented with clever carvings, representing the planets, as well as with well-cut figures of lions and elephants; these prove that the plastic as well as the mechanical arts had made greater progress in Orissa than they had contemporaneously in England. There used to be ruins also in the ancient city of Cuttack, which indicates a remote antiquity, as well as an advanced civilization. [In short, there can be no doubt that the country had sunk from a flourishing kingdom to something approaching a wilderness. It has gone through various religious phases—has been Buddhist, is now Hindoo, in the low lands; whilst in the hills is a worse heathenism than either. Revolution after revolution swept over Orissa, changing the aspect of the country materially; still it maintained a name among the states of Hindostan till the year 1558, when its sovereignty ceased, and it became an outlying province of the Great Mogul's empire. Upon the breaking up of this powerful state, the more valuable portions of the country were seized by the Nizam of Hydrabad. Change, however, succeeded change. European settlements began to be made in Hindostan, and Christian masters succeeded Mahomedan, Buddhists, and Brahmins. A part of the country long known as the Northern Circars became a French colony. The French made a vigorous effort to drive the English, who had also made trading settlements in the same part of the world, out of India, but did not succeed. The Mahrattas had seized upon part of Orissa in 1740, but were forced to surrender this to England in 1803. The result of our struggle with France for supremacy in India is well known.]

Almost at the commencement of the century, the soldiers of the East India Company were marched into Orissa; but arrangements being made by which the chiefs agreed to pay tribute, the only warlike operation was that performed by a detachment of 7000 men sent against a strong fort, commanded by one of the native princes, at the head of a numerous army, composed of Ooryas, a brave native race, that partly subdued the Khonds; but the English rule was soon established, and the principal chiefs and princes paid tribute to the amount of 118,687 rupees to the Anglo-Indian Government at Calcutta, the said Government stipulating to perform certain services for the advantage of the said country—one maintaining the river embankments amounted in the year 1814 to 40,514 rupees. The princes were to retain a more than nominal independence, for the power of life and death remained in their hands, and they could levy war against their neighbours without seeking or obtaining the permission of the British Government. So long as they paid their annual tribute they did pretty much as they pleased.

The hill districts of Orissa, termed in their language Maliah, from the Sanscrit Mala, a garland, so called from the abundance of jungle, are peopled generally by Khonds, or Kui, as they call themselves. There are, however, other wild tribes, named respectively Koles, Gonds, and Sourahs. It is, however, chiefly with the Khonds that I have had to do. These are all subjects, to a certain extent, of the Rajah or prince ruling over the lowland territory in their neighbourhood. The relation they owe and the obedience they yield their Rajahs will appear more clearly as my narrative proceeds.

Much of the Khond territory is little better than a wilderness, although it comprises some thousand square miles, where valleys and stretches of level ravines occasionally intersect the forest of thick brushwood. Wherever the land is cleared, it is cultivated for rice or dhall, a kind of bean much prized for food. The highest elevation is not more than three thousand feet. The ascent to the Khond hills, from Goomsur up the Khoorminghia Pass, is upwards of two thousand feet, and there is another sharp ascent from Serampur to Gûddapur.

Coarse grass and shrubs cover these acclivities,

where no attempt at cultivation has been made. Beds of rocky torrents occur frequently, but running streams are sometimes found, such as the Bugundi, which waters the valleys of the Maji Deso, and feeds the Mahanuddy river, near Sohnpore; in short, as in all mountain lands, there is abundance of water, though it is turned to less account, by the inhabitants of the villages, for agricultural purposes than it might be.

The Khonds consider themselves the lords and owners of the soil, and no tribe will ever part with land for any consideration whatever. The property in a single tree will be tenaciously defended for centuries, and never yielded save in obedience to overwhelming necessity. Their villages, of which I will say more by-and-bye, vary greatly in extent and population, sometimes consisting of a single street with a few families, and sometimes of a community numbering three to four hundred.

As a race, the Khonds are not remarkable; the men are often well formed, and in every way superior to the women, the latter being short in figure, and very plain in feature. To European ideas they are certainly most repulsive. If, as some have asserted, they are the descendants of the Indo-Tartar tribes that fled for refuge to the mountainous forests from the pursuit of the destroyer, I can only say that they have contrived to lose all the intellectual and nearly all the physical attributes by which these people were characterized. The Khonds are a degenerate race, with all the ignorance and superstition of savages.

Although it cannot be affirmed that the Khonds turn the resources of their country to the best account, still they are not a slothful race, as they bring very much more of the land into tillage than is required to supply their wants. The head man of each village usually acts as chief merchant, buying and bartering whenever he can profitably do so. If no travelling merchants pass through the villages and purchase their produce, then the Khonds carry it in baskets, slung at each end of a pole, to neighbouring fairs and markets in the low country. In this way, mustard, castor oil seeds, ginger, turmeric, sweet potatoes, yams, plantains, citron, gourds, pumpkins, beans, tobacco, are reared and sold.

The cotton shrub is abundant everywhere, but turned to no account. I have heard it asserted that cotton might be extensively cultivated on the Khond hills, but I am not competent to give a decided opinion. The presence of the cotton shrub almost everywhere certainly favours the idea, but if very careful European supervision is needful successfully to cultivate this plant, then I do not think very much of it can be expected from the hill tracts of Orissa.

Constant exposure in this climate would soon prove fatal to any European constitution, and this circumstance alone must prevent these obscure districts from ever becoming the seats of prosperous industry or great commercial enterprise.

Oranges and lemons abound, but generally of a very inferior description.

The Khond usually carries a long staff, but when armed he wears a turban ornamented with a showy crest of feathers, and a strong cloth encircling his loins; he carries a bow and arrows, and a battle-axe with the blade in two divisions. He marches to battle singing, shouting, and brandishing his battle-axe, most commonly under the influence of strong potations. The matchlock and shield are the favourite weapons of the people inhabiting the Southern district; but the curious and formidable battle-axe seems most relied on by the heroes of Boad and Goomsur.

They are not without musical instruments, of a rude kind, with which they contrive to make a good deal of noise at their festivals, drums and trumpets being most in request. There is also a lute, of two wires, stretched over a gourd, and a shepherd's pipe. Their concerts are pastoral as well as elegiac, the instruments accompanying rustic and marriage songs—the ceremonial of the priest, and the amatory confession of the lover. Something in the way of verse is

OORYAH (HINDOO) CHIEF OF KHONDISTAN: KHOND WEAPONS IN THE BACKGROUND.

attempted, with pretensions to rhythm and metre; but the composition scarcely amounts to poetry. The poet chants rather than sings, accompanied by a player on the two-stringed lute, something after the fashion of penillion singing in Wales, only that the Welsh bard is much better off for music. Nevertheless, the effect is wild, and not unpleasing, even to refined European ears.

Probably these performances have degenerated, like the people who flock to them, and are vestiges of musical and poetical excellence that flourished in the ancient kingdom—the ruins of a lost civilization, that distinguished Orissa in a far distant age. Nothing, however, very flattering to either Ooryah or Khond can be made out, either of the melodies or of the versification. They are as barbarous as the country and the people.

The toilet of the Khond does not require much attention or expense, seeing that his entire costume usually consists of a piece of coarse cloth worn round his loins—a narrow strip, woven in the country, with the ends of a gay colour, having a smart fringe. The head-dress, however, is a much more elaborate affair. The hair being worn very long, is drawn and rolled into the fashion of a horn, that projects from between the eyes, and is wrapped in a piece of red cloth, decorated with bright feathers. In this the

Khond generally places his comb, pipe, and other little domestic requisites.

The Bissoi, or chief, and his family, are much better off for clothing; indeed, he not unfrequently assumes robes of state, varying from a red blanket with a gaudy fringe, to a dress of honour of silk or other expensive fabric, which he has received as a present from the Sirkar, or European agent of Government.

The dress of the Khond women varies from that of the males. Nothing is worn over the bosom, and the cloth that is fastened round their middle seldom reaches to the knee. Brass rings ornament the ears of both sexes, sometimes the nostrils also; necklaces of the same metal, or a string of glass beads, adorn the neck, and heavy brass bands the arms. In short, such ornaments are in so much favour, that they are almost as greatly prized as strips of red cloth. Copper coins are sometimes used for personal decoration; generally, however, for children, when strung together by way of necklace; but there is very little money in the villages, and in some, its use being unknown, it is often refused in payment for articles of barter.

Their ordinary diet is mostly vegetable—dhâl and rice, boiled into a broth or porridge; but the hunters eat freely of what they kill of wild game, rarely slaughtering domestic animals for food. They distil intoxicating liquors from rice and from the mahwa flowers, in which they indulge, as well as in the fermented juice of the palm. They also smoke tobacco universally, and at every opportunity that permits of the indulgence.

The principal Hindoo Zemindars of the districts comprising the hill tracts, maintain little courts at their respective seats of government—as at Boad, Duspullah, Patna, Kimedy, Guddapoor, &c. There is an appearance of feudal vassalage and rule maintained by these petty monarchs, who are surrounded by a staff of ministers and other officials, who manage the affairs of the district. These Rajahs and their officers are the greatest possible sticklers in all matters of court ceremony. If one of them visits a village chief, he is met by the latter, accompanied by all the followers he can muster, and saluted with a low obeisance. The village chief then presents the feudal tribute, washes his superior's feet, and escorts him with music to his house, before which a spot has been swept and purified. Here are placed a lamp and a vessel full of water, in which a small branch of the mango-tree is immersed. The wife of the village chief then brings some rice, and showing it to the illustrious visitor, describes a circle round his head with joined palms; which done, she throws the rice away, and sprinkles the water on the roof of the house.

He is then escorted to a house set apart for him, where he resides, his charge being borne by the village community. Matchlocks are fired off, and the Khond subjects of the Rajah assemble to give him welcome. Should a beast of the chase be presented, he receives it, and distributes it at his pleasure.

In former times, before our Government came in contact with these Rajahs, a fixed sum was paid by all these hill villages as tribute, which has now almost ceased, although the Rajahs continue to exercise a certain influence; and I always sought their aid as a preliminary measure. The importance which I attached to their co-operation in suppressing human sacrifices amongst their hill subjects necessarily increased their own importance, of which they are very jealous, and I did not generally find them inaccessible to arguments that held out a prospect of personal advantage.

The Ooryah language is, of course, spoken by these Rajahs, who can only understand their Khond subjects through interpreters. The Khond language did not exist as a written dialect until Captain Frye, at my request, reduced it to a written form, using the Ooryah character; and there are now several little works which are made use of in the schools established in Khondistan. The Khond language is capable of much force of expression, as I have had frequent occasion to notice at the many "councils" I have held with the tribes. The orator, on such occasions, commences his address in a low voice, gradually warming with his subject, into which he seems to throw his whole soul, and rapidly jerking out a succession of sharp utterances. He is regarded with deep attention by all assembled. At the conclusion of a long harangue, the speaker glances round with a somewhat frightened look, and a general murmuring takes place in the assembly.

An appeal has recently been put forth by the missionaries in Orissa, for assistance in carrying out the conversion of the Khonds, and two of their number have devoted themselves to this work. I heartily wish, in common with every Christian both in England and India, for the success of an object so desirable. I regret that these gentlemen have resolved to dwell in the low country, and expect the Khonds to come to them; but I trust this is only preparatory to a lengthy annual residence in the hill tracts, and constant visits to the hill villages. Khondistan may be traversed in winter with comparative impunity; and I hope that the missionaries will endeavour to acclimatise themselves during this season—for, without their personal presence and constant supervision, the hill tribes are not likely to become converts, and certainly will not remain so, should they be induced to profess Christianity?

Other characteristics of these wild tribes will be described in the account I have given, in subsequent chapters, of each province I visited.

CHAPTER II.

THE KHONDS DESCENDANTS OF THE ABORIGINES—THEIR OORYAH RULERS —PRIDE OF ANCESTRY—ANNUAL TRIBUTE FROM THE HILL CHIEFS TO THE ANGLO-INDIAN GOVERNMENT—DESCRIPTION OF GOOMSUR AND ITS RAJAH—STRECKARAH BUNGE DEFIES THE BRITISH GOVERNMENT —HIS OVERTHROW AND SUBSEQUENT REVOLT—HIS SON'S REBELLION —MILITARY FORCE SENT AGAINST HIM—I AM APPOINTED ASSISTANT AND SECRETARY TO THE POLITICAL AGENT—A SEVEN YEARS' CAMPAIGN IN THE HILLS—THE DORA BISSYE—CONQUEST OF GOOMSUR— CASUALTIES BY THE WAR.

CHAPTER II.

THE appearance, habits, dress, and other characteristics of the Khonds point out these people as descendants from the aboriginal inhabitants of the country.* On the eastern side, Telingahs, Ooryahs, &c., have driven them from the narrow fertile belt between the mountains and the sea; while on the western side of the Ghauts, the Gonds from Nagpore have encroached to the very foot of the hills. At present villages of both Ooryahs and Khonds are scattered throughout the wide and dense forests of Patna, Kalahundy, Jeypore, Kariall, and Nowaguddah. No Khonds, however, are to be found westward of Kariall and Nowaguddah. The space over which this wild tribe is scattered, extends from the north of the Mahanuddy to as far south as the river Godavery.

Between these two points, the country is divided into forty or fifty petty principalities, ruled over by chiefs of the Ooryah caste. For although the

* Hill's Reports, 1838.

Khonds, who inhabit only the mountain ranges, profess to be very independent, they in reality are subject to these low country rulers, and, in one way or another, acknowledge a certain kind of submission. Sometimes, it is true, the tribes quarrel with their lowland chief, and then they literally

> "Rush like a torrent down upon the plains,
> Sweeping the flocks and herds."

On such occasions, the Rajah, or ruler, if he be strong enough, makes reprisals ; if not, he implores the British Government in India to interpose their good offices to allay the feud. The Rajahs, or Orissa chieftains, pretend that they keep the Khonds under subjection, but I know that frequently the reverse is more nearly the fact.

These chieftains are generally uneducated men, devoid of all mental culture. They are exceedingly proud and haughty, claiming, I believe, justly, a very ancient origin. Many lay claim to a fabulous descent, and point to their coat of arms as indicating the animal or object from which their ancestors sprung. The Rajah of Goomsur, for example, had a peacock, another prince a snake, and a third a bamboo tree ; and these cognizances are no small source of pride.

But with all such childish vanity, these petty rulers are in truth an abjectly degraded class. Many, from early debauchery, and the unbridled indulgence of their passions, become completely imbecile. They are generally surrounded by artful, cunning men and designing relatives, who promote their excesses in every way, in order the better to maintain over them an influence which they can turn to their own profit. It is not then surprising that amongst this class of men feebleness of character prevails. Nevertheless they are to be pitied ; they have not yet been taught the value of a moral obligation, and have never had the means of discriminating between good and evil. Born and bred in an atmosphere of vice, they become comparatively enervated before they have attained manhood. The welfare of the people committed to their charge is never allowed for one moment to interfere with their gratifications, however objectionable.

From each of these rulers the State exacts an annual tribute, varying from one to eight thousand pounds. Is it to be wondered that such men are generally unable to pay the demand of Government ? The State presses again and again for the tribute money, which has been allowed to fall into arrears; and if the delinquent Rajah, after due time has been allowed him, fails to raise the amount, the revenue officers of Government administer the estate until such time as the debt is paid off ; but where the arrears are very heavy, and there is no hope of their being paid in the usual course, then the estate is sold to liquidate the balance due, the Government usually becoming the purchaser.

I will, in a few words, sketch the history of the small Palatinate of Goomsur, because it was owing to the deposition of the reigning prince, and the consequent annexation of his country to the British dominions, that we first became acquainted with the superstition that formed so striking a feature in the native character.

Goomsur reckons about four hundred square miles, one half of which is primeval forest, the other cleared and well cultivated land. In 1783, this little principality was ruled over by a Rajah named Vikramah Bunge, and from him a yearly tribute of five thousand pounds was demanded by the Government. It is almost superfluous to say that he never paid it. When at last the patience of the supreme power in India was exhausted, his estate was taken from him and placed in the hands of his brother, Lutshmunnah Bunge.

This man had more sense than falls to the lot of ordinary Rajahs; he called to his aid all the financiers of his little kingdom, and gave them virtual control of the revenue. They in return guaranteed the amount due to the State; and, so far as I know, there were never any arrears during his lifetime, though there is reason to believe that the control exercised by the Native bankers, both over the Rajah in particular and the country in general, did not give universal satisfaction. Be this as it may, the Rajah died in peace, and his son, Streckarah Bunge reigned in his stead.

Most chequered was the career of this native prince. He viewed apparently with disgust the dominion exercised by the money-dealers, and threw himself into the arms of the priests. Under the pretext of a pilgrimage to some holy shrine, he made an apparent abdication of his power in favour of his son, Dhunagi Bunge. But this was merely one of those mad freaks in which such fanatics often indulge; for, after an absence of a few years, he suddenly returned to his country, and, without any just cause, expelled his son, and resumed the reins of government.

Nor was this all he did; for no sooner had he reinstalled himself in office, than he determined to signalise his advent to power by an act of mingled boldness and defiance. He intimated his determination henceforward to pay no tribute money whatever, and thus magnanimously threw down the gauntlet to the paramount power in India.

This challenge did not long remain unanswered. Troops were rapidly poured into his country, and in a very short time this unruly Rajah was transformed into a private gentleman. It is impossible to imagine any adequate motive that could have induced him to provoke the storm which he had no means of resisting; but the fact is, that these little potentates seldom, never perhaps, act under the inspiration of reason, but simply as impulse dictates; and the result is certain—they are defeated and dethroned.

The supreme Government then resolved to allow this foolish man to meditate in retirement on his folly, and to replace at the head of affairs the son in whose favour the father had previously abdicated. This was accordingly done, and Dhunagi Bunge once more directed the vessel of the state. But he was as bad a pilot as his father, and altogether a worse man. Under his rule, crime succeeded crime, and anarchy and confusion were rife. The Anglo-Indian Government again interfered, and so serious were the charges preferred against Dhunagi Bunge that it became necessary again to depose, as well as to imprison him.

Then came the father's turn again, and for the last time; he was recalled from banishment, and remounted the throne, but, like other illustrious princes, he had in exile neither learnt nor forgotten anything; and after a very short possession of power, he failed to pay the stipulated tribute, again revolted, again was overpowered, and subsequently was sent to expiate his crimes and follies in a distant land.

Once more the British Government gave the son a

chance of retrieving his past errors—released him from confinement, and reinstalled him as ruler of Goomsur. In fact, this poor harassed district was in a constant state of oscillation between father and son, who alternately reigned and were deposed. The great disinclination of the government to adopt the only alternative of annexing the country, had led them to hope, almost against hope, that the repeated and severe lessons that had been taught both father and son would have had the desired effect of endowing them with a little wisdom. But Rajahs are past teaching.

The first use the son, Dhunagi Bunge, made of his return to power, was to hoist the standard of rebellion and defy the paramount power to do its worst. *Quem Deus vult perdere prius dementat* was true, if ever, in this lamentable case. With common prudence Dhunagi Bunge might have been ruler of Goomsur to this hour; for the extreme mercy shown him by the Governor-General, in so frequently pardoning his crimes, and replacing him in power, abundantly testified the desire of the Government to do all that was possible to preserve this little kingdom to its legitimate rulers. Of course all things have their limit, and this extravagant act of defiance was the last drop that made the cup of government indignation to overflow. A decree went forth for the complete subjugation of the country, and an adequate army was appointed for that purpose. The Rajah determined on a fierce resistance in his mountain fastnesses, and thither he betook himself, calling upon his wild and warlike tribes of Khonds to aid him in maintaining his rights.

A large force, chiefly composed of troops from Madras, was assembled under the command of General Sir Henry Taylor. The Hon. Mr. Russell was named Political Agent, and very extensive powers were vested in him. I was appointed to be his assistant and secretary, and took an active part throughout the whole campaign, which extended over two years.

The Rajah's summons to his tribes of Khonds was readily responded to. Their great chief, and the foremost supporter of the Rajah at that time, was the Dora Bissye, who was regarded as the leader of the rebellion on the hills. By his able and wily counsels the Rajah was chiefly guided, and it must be admitted that he gave our troops very great annoyance. No doubt the war would have dragged on much longer, had it not been for the treachery of some of his own adherents, and the hostility of the bordering tribes.

In a very short time Mr. Russell became acquainted with the names, connexions, and haunts of all the Khond leaders; but even then we should not have been able to track them in their wild jungles, had they not been surrendered by the tribes themselves, who, unable to continue the contest longer, sued for peace and forgiveness by delivering them up. A large number of the rebel leaders were executed; the unhappy Rajah was hunted from place to place, and finally died at a little mountain fortress. The Dora Bissye became a state prisoner, and was alive only a few years ago at the Fort of Gooty, in Madras.

He was a very remarkable man, and when he found the fortune of war so much against him, escaped into the territories of a neighbouring prince, the Rajah of Ungool, by whom he was subsequently delivered up to the British authorities, on the condition that his life should be spared. All the objects contemplated by the Government were accomplished, and the whole country became part of the British territory.

The two years' campaign was of unexampled severity. We had no knowledge of the country, were frequently cut off from all supplies, and suffered fearfully from the pestilential nature of the climate. Hardship, privation and peril were the lot of all who took part in this second Goomsur war. The casualties from the bows and arrows of the Khonds were not very great; but on one or two occasions they came in force upon weak detachments of our troops, who had lost themselves in the unknown mountain defiles, and then no mercy was shown—they hacked them to pieces. We lost in this way two European officers, who were accompanying a small escort down a narrow mountain pass, where they were surrounded by the Khonds and slaughtered.

On the termination of the war all the regular troops were withdrawn from the hills, and the tribes remained under the rule of chiefs, for the most part appointed by the Anglo-Indian Government; hence we were in a favourable position, as these men had seen and felt our strength and power, and were likely to render us substantial service.

CHAPTER III.

MOUNTAINOUS REGION KNOWN AS KHONDISTAN—HARDSHIPS ENDURED BY ENGLISH OFFICERS CAMPAIGNING IN SO WILD A DISTRICT—THE KHONDS AND THEIR LANGUAGE—LORD ELPHINSTONE'S DESCRIPTION OF THEM—THEIR SUPERSTITIOUS PRACTICES—DRINKING AND HUNTING—ATTACKING A BEAR—NATIVE DRESS—SINGULAR HEAD-DRESS—MARTIAL COSTUME—COMBAT OF TRIBES—KHOND WOMEN AND THEIR ORNAMENTS—ABDUCTION—MARRIAGE—BELIEF IN MAGIC—TIGER WITCHES.

CHAPTER III.

THE harassing operations to which I have referred in the preceding chapter first brought us into contact with the wild and warlike inhabitants of the table-land of the great chain of hills extending north and south from the Mahanuddy to the Godavery.

These mountains are about two hundred miles distant from the sea, and from two to three thousand feet above it. They are almost inaccessible, and in 1836 there was not a single tolerable approach known to us. We had to scramble up their rugged sides as best we could, and very weary work it was. The common bamboo, with the damur-tree, is found in profusion, and covers the elevations on every side. Partridge, peacock, jungle-fowl, and other descriptions of game, are everywhere met with; and the larger animals, tigers, panthers, bears, wild buffaloes, are numerous.

When once the summit is reached, the change from the low country is very striking. The eye beholds a well-watered and open country of table-land, producing luxuriantly rice, oil seeds, turmeric, and sometimes large crops of dhall (a kind of pea) and millet. Of the science of agriculture the people know absolutely nothing; they exhaust the soil with unintermitted crops, until the land is barren, then they abandon their fields, and clear fresh jungle for future crops.

The inhabitants of the Orissa range of hills are called respectively Khonds, Gonds, and Sourahs. The language of these three tribes is totally distinct, and the two latter are not addicted to the practice of human sacrifice.

The Khonds bear no resemblance whatever to the inhabitants of the plains. They are of a much darker complexion, strongly bronzed, and their language differs from that of all the other tribes, and is not in the least comprehended by their lowland neighbours. I should imagine that they had been driven from the plains centuries ago by successive conquerors, and had sought a refuge in these distant hills; for though their language is a distinct dialect, there are words, having both a Telingah, Canarese, and Ooryah origin.

"Indeed, there seems reason to suppose," Lord Elphinstone has stated, "that these wild tribes who now inhabit the most inaccessible parts of the mountains and forests are the descendants of the aborigines of the whole country. In their religion we find traces of the primitive elemental worship of the Vedas, before it was overlaid by the superstructure which now almost conceals it from our eyes, as well as from those of the generality of Hindoos themselves; and it would be curious if the impious superstition (human sacrifice), which we would now endeavour to eradicate, can trace its origin to the purer and simpler form of adoration which we have been taught to consider the ancient religion of India, as compared with the relatively modern mythology which has sprung from and overgrown it."

Much of this, of course, is mere speculation, and it may readily be conceived how difficult it was to acquire accurate information of the religion of a people who had no written language. Sacrifice is the foundation of their religion, and, saving a very few tribes, the Khonds generally propitiated their deity, always a malevolent being, with human offerings. I am aware that a complete system of mythology has been devised for them, but much has been introduced of which the Khonds know nothing whatever.

As a rule, they are generally active, wiry, and agile, while but imperfectly acquainted with the value of cleanliness. Every man carries an axe, and the far greater part of them a bow and arrow also. They have never adopted the matchlock, sword, or shield, which their Ooryah chiefs or Bissoi always carry; and this is the more singular, as these weapons are very superior to those used by the Khonds. They are excessively devoted to liquor and tobacco. The fruit of the Mowah tree affords them a very strong spirit, of which they drink deeply, as well as of the fermented juice of the feathery palm.

They are passionately fond of hunting, and pursue the sport with an eagerness and ardour found only amongst people of the forest. Their hunting season opens about April, at which period they burn the underwood and rank grass of the jungle, an operation which drives the wild beasts from their lairs to seek a refuge in the unburnt forest. While thus moving from one point to another, they are pursued by the Khonds, who are exceedingly expert at tracking game and running down wounded animals.

The following instance occurred to Lieut. McNeill when out bear shooting, accompanied by some Khonds, who had been rescued from sacrifice. He had posted himself in a favourable position one moonlight night, when a bear came up, but owing to the uncertain light, for the moon was not very bright, he only wounded the beast slightly; it made off at once right across the rice fields in the open plain, with the intention of seeking shelter in the neighbouring hills, without allowing time for the adjustment of the sight for a second shot.

The Khonds had started at full speed in pursuit, to cut off the animal's retreat to the hills; they soon placed themselves between the bear and the hills, and then with axe in hand they resolutely attacked him, and literally hacked him to pieces in less time than it has taken to narrate this adventure. The axes used were certainly formidable weapons, but it requires more than ordinary courage to attack a savage bear with such instruments as these, by moonlight, and on broken ground.

If, while hunting, an elk or other large game is wounded, the measure of his "gotteru" or slot is taken; they then have an admitted right to pursue to any place, either within or without their own boundaries, until the animal is killed or captured. A division of the quarry is now made in accordance with well-established usage—so many portions to the hunters, so many to the villagers on whose land it has been killed, and not unfrequently the Rajah, or low country chief, comes in for a share. In the event of any dispute regarding the identity of the pursued animal, the measure of the first slot is produced, and received as conclusive.

During the hunting season universal drunkenness and revelry prevail. The men gather together in little knots, and absorb their fermented juices until they are perfectly besotted.

Their clothes consist merely of a few yards of coarse cotton cloth bound round the loins, ornamented with a separate piece striped with red, and dangling down behind like a tail. Their thick black hair, wound round and round their heads, is fastened in front by a knot, over which is tied a strip of red or other cloth.

In their hair they invariably stick three or four cigars, very simply formed by rolling a green leaf into a conical shape, and filling it with their coarse chopped tobacco leaf.

It is only, however, when they go out to battle, and tribe meets tribe in hostile array, that they adorn themselves with all their finery. Then they swathe their heads in thick folds of cotton cloth, with peacocks' feathers waving in defiance, cover their bodies with pieces of skins of bears or elks; and proud indeed is the warrior who can sport over all a couple of yards of red cloth.

I once witnessed two tribes, each numbering about three hundred men, drawn up in battle array. On this occasion I prevented any serious results. They had already been three days engaged in the preliminaries of the fight, for many ceremonies are gone through "ere comes the tug of war."

Champions from either side perform war dances

between the hostile armies, which are accompanied by offensive and insulting epithets, and each side challenges and abuses the other. At last they are sufficiently excited, and from words the dancers come to blows. A general *mêlée* ensues, which is rarely attended with great loss of life, and at night the opposing parties draw off to their respective quarters, only to recommence the strife on the following day.

The Khond women are as scantily clad as the men. They partake of the prevailing weakness of their sex —an intense love of ornaments and finery. Coloured beads are highly prized and generally used, as well as a rude and heavy description of brass bracelet worn on their arms and ankles. As a class, as I have said, they are far from good-looking, and their standard of morality is not, I regret to say, very elevated ; hence arise endless quarrels among them. The Khonds regard the abduction of a woman by a man of another tribe as a common insult to them all, and unless reparation be made to the injured husband, war is declared against the tribe of the abducting party, and all who are more or less distantly connected with the disputants are drawn into the quarrel.

Marriages are usually celebrated at the hunting time, and then in almost every village may be heard the sound of their shrill musical instruments.

Many of their customs bearing on this rite are peculiar. On one occasion, whilst taking an evening ride, I heard loud cries proceeding from a village close at hand. Fearing some serious quarrel, I rode to the spot, and there I saw a man bearing away upon his back something enveloped in an ample covering of scarlet cloth ; he was surrounded by twenty or thirty young fellows, and by them protected from the desperate attacks made on him by a party of young women. On seeking an explanation of this novel scene, I was told that the man had just been married, and his precious burthen was his blooming bride, whom he was conveying to his own village. Her youthful friends, as it appears is the custom, were seeking to regain possession of her, and hurled stones and bamboos at the head of the devoted bridegroom, until he reached the confines of his own village. Then the tables were turned, the bride was fairly won, and off her young friends scampered, screaming and laughing, but not relaxing their speed until they reached their own village.

The Khonds are firm believers in magic, and frequently attribute death or misfortune of any kind to enchantment. They believe that witches have the faculty of transforming themselves into tigers, and are then called "Pulta Bag." This belief is very similar to the superstition of the peasants of Normandy or Brittany, who imagine that certain people have power to change themselves into wolves, and very often have so changed themselves for the purpose of frightening others and doing mischief. I had heard often of these "Pulta Bags," and one example came under my own observation.

Whilst examining some magisterial cases, I observed a crowd approaching with two women in front, guarded by three or four armed men. In due time they were brought before me, and charged by a Beniah (one of a tribe of Khonds inhabiting the slopes of the mountains) with having transformed themselves into tigers, and killed and carried off his son. His story was:—

"I went in the evening to the jungle near my village accompanied by my son, to gather fire-wood. We were engaged in doing so when a tiger sprung upon my son and carried him off. I pursued, shouting and making as much noise as I could, when suddenly, on turning the shoulder of a rock, I saw these two women standing on the top of it. The thing was now clear—the Pulta Bag, alarmed at my shouts and close pursuit, concealed the body of my son and resumed their original shape. I took them prisoners to my village, where they confessed to what I now charge them with. Here they are, ask them."

I did so, and to my surprise both women acknowledged that the Beniah Khond's story was true—they had killed his son, and had power to transform themselves into tigers. Determined to undeceive the people as to this extraordinary belief, I told the women that I would release them on condition of their transforming themselves into tigers in my presence, which, to the horror of all, they agreed to do if taken to a neighbouring jungle. This I ordered to be done; when, seeing no mode of escape, they threw themselves on the ground, imploring mercy and pardon, and confessing the imposture. They stated that they were poor, and lived by imposing on the credulity of the villagers, who supplied them with food and clothing whenever they chose to demand it, in order to secure themselves and cattle from their depredations in the form of a Pulta Bag. Some of the people were convinced of the imposture, but the majority were disappointed that the supposed witches were not burnt or drowned.

CHAPTER IV.

KHOND VILLAGES AND HOUSES—RICE CULTIVATION—VILLAGE AUTHORITIES—THE BISSOI—AGRICULTURAL IMPLEMENTS—SYSTEM OF HUMAN SACRIFICE—THE EARTH GODDESS AND BLOOD RED GOD OF BATTLE—POSSIAPOES, OR ADOPTED CHILDREN—MR. RUSSELL'S REPORT OF THE CEREMONIES PERFORMED DURING A HUMAN SACRIFICE—ACCOUNT FURNISHED BY MR. RICKETT'S COMMISSIONER AT CULLACK—PRICE OF VICTIMS—CONTRADICTORY STATEMENTS—ATTENTION OF THE ANGLO-INDIAN GOVERNMENT ATTRACTED—MY APPOINTMENT AS POLITICAL AGENT AND MAGISTRATE AMONG THE SACRIFICING TRIBES.

CHAPTER IV.

Khond communities are divided into districts and villages. Each is formed of a union of the latter, and called a Mootah ; and these again, united, form a district. Their villages vary in size from twenty to eighty houses, well and substantially built, and in every way are superior to those of the low country. The timber used for building purposes is the Damur tree, which is found in abundance in these mountains, and the axe is the only tool they use to fashion it into shape. They roof their houses with bamboo, and then thatch them over as thickly as possible with grass. The village consists usually of one long street, with a rough kind of palisade at either end. Clusters of villages are always grouped together, for the double purpose of defence and cultivation.

Rice is their great staple, and these people bestow great pains upon its cultivation. The fields are formed in a succession of terraces, to which water is conducted with no mean skill. Adjoining each village, is invariably to be seen the common tobacco-plant, a rough, coarse, strong leaf, indispensable, however, to gratify the Khond appetite. It is regarded by them as one of the most necessary articles of existence.

Each village has its own chief, or Mulleko, and with him is joined an officer, called Digaloo, or interpreter, of the Panoo caste, a race most useful to the Khond tribes, though they regard them as greatly their inferiors. I shall have to speak of these Panoos, as the agents in the detestable traffic of human victims. They transact all business for the Khonds, who consider it beneath their dignity to barter or traffic, and who regard as base and plebeian all who are not either warriors or tillers of the soil.

Districts again are governed by a chief of the Ooryah extraction, and named the Bissoi. These men are Hindoos, and are usually descended from some daring adventurer, whose fallen fortunes had driven him to the hills, where, with his band of retainers, he had been warmly welcomed by the mountain tribes, as the Khonds regard these Hindoo warriors as much more capable of ruling over them, and especially of leading them to battle, than any of their own tribe.

They have no caste prejudices, such as obtain universally on the plains of India; they eat almost anything, but they do not drink milk, though they can assign no reason for their abstinence.

Their implements of husbandry are very primitive, as they merely scratch the ground with a rough wooden plough, drawn either by buffaloes or small oxen. Their breed of cattle is very inferior; indeed, the worst I ever saw in any land. Sheep are extremely scarce, but goats abound in every part of their mountains, and some descriptions afford very excellent and nutritious meat.

It was there, amongst these hill tribes, that we discovered, during the war, with mingled horror and surprise, that a system of human sacrifice, aggravated by the cruel manner of its performance, existed almost universally. This revolting rite had been handed down through successive generations; it was regarded as a national and most necessary duty, so darkened were their minds by the gross delusions of ignorance and superstition.

In the hill countries of Goomsur and Boad, the human blood is offered to the earth goddess, under the effigy of a bird, in the hope of thus obtaining abundant crops, averting calamity, and insuring general prosperity.

In Chinna Kimedy this deity is represented by an elephant, but the purposes for which the sacrifice is offered are the same as in Goomsur.

In Jeypore the "blood-red god of battle, Maneck-soroo" (thus they style him), is the deity whom they seek to propitiate by human victims. Thus, on the eve of a battle, or when a new fort, or even an important village is to be built, or when danger of any kind is to be averted, this sanguinary being must be propitiated with human blood.

Irrespective of the sacrifices offered by the community as a body, it is not an uncommon thing for private individuals to make special offerings on their own account, in order to secure the attainment of any particular object.

Both the motive and manner of sacrifice differ amongst the various tribes; the rite itself, however, is performed with invariable cruelty. The victims, called Meriah, must be bought with a price. This condition is essential. They may be of any age, sex, or caste; but adults are most esteemed, because they are the most costly, and therefore the most acceptable to the deity. They are sometimes purchased from their parents or relations, when these have fallen into poverty, or in seasons of famine; but they are most commonly stolen from the plains by professed kidnappers of the Panoo caste.

These Panoos are base and sordid miscreants, who, without the excuse of superstition or ignorance, carry on a profitable trade in the blood of their fellow-men. Unfortunate people of the low country are decoyed into the hills by these miscreants, and then sold to the Khonds for Meriah sacrifices. Their guilt admits of no palliation, and no mercy is ever shown them when they are brought up for punishment.

In some cases Meriah women are allowed to live until they have borne children to Khond fathers; these children are then reared for sacrifice, but never put to death in the village of their birth; to avoid this they are exchanged for children born under similar conditions in other villages. Meriahs are always treated with marked kindness, and are seldom subjected to any restraint. Money is rarely used in the purchase of Meriah victims, the price agreed on being usually paid in cattle, pigs, goats, brass vessels or ornaments, and sometimes in saffron, wax, and other products of the hills.

The sacrifice, to be efficacious, must be celebrated in public before the assembled people.

I may just allude here to another class of persons who are purchased by the Khonds, or procured by them for adoption into their families, as helps in household affairs, and in field labours. These are called Possia Poes, and are usually obtained when young. They run little or no risk of being sacrificed, and very often marry into the families of their purchasers, and in the course of time merge into the general population.

Of the manner of sacrifice in Goomsur I cannot do better than quote from the interesting report of Mr. Russell, whose secretary I was during the war; he says:—

"In the Maliahs (hill tracts) of Goomsur the sacrifice is offered annually to Tado Pennor, the earth god, under the effigy of a peacock, with the view of propitiating the deity to grant favourable crops. The Zani, or priest, who may be of any caste, officiates at the sacrifice, but he performs the 'Pooga' (offering of flowers, incense, &c.) to the idol, through the medium of the Zoomba, who must be a Khond boy under seven years of age, and who is fed and clothed at the public expense, eats alone, and is subjected to no act deemed impure.

"For a month prior to the sacrifice, there is much feasting, intoxication, and dancing round the Meriah (victim), who is adorned with garlands, &c. On the day before the performance of the barbarous rite, he is stupefied with toddy, and is made to sit, or is bound at the bottom of a post, bearing the effigy above described. The assembled multitude then dance round to music, and addressing the earth, say, 'O God, we offer this sacrifice to you; give us good crops, seasons, and health;' after which they address the victim. 'We bought you with a price, and did not seize you; now we sacrifice you according to custom, and no sin rests with us.'

"On the following day, the Meriah being again intoxicated, and anointed with oil, each individual present touches the anointed part, and wipes the oil on his own head. All then march in procession round the village and its boundaries, preceded by music, bearing the victim in their arms. On returning to the post, which is always placed near the village idol, called Zacari Penoo, represented by three stones, a hog is killed in sacrifice, and the blood being allowed to flow into a pit prepared for the purpose, the Meriah, who has been previously made senseless from intoxication, is seized and thrown in, and his face pressed down till he is suffocated in the bloody mire. The Zani then cuts a piece of flesh from the body, and buries it near the village idol, as an offering to the earth. All the people then follow his example, but carry the bloody prize to their own villages, where part of the flesh is buried near the village idol, and part on the boundaries of the village. The head of the victim remains unmutilated, and with the bare bones is buried in the bloody pit.

"After this horrid ceremony has been completed, a buffalo calf is brought to the post, and, his four feet having been cut off, is left there till the following day. Women, dressed in male attire and armed as men, then drink, dance, and sing round the spot; the calf is killed and eaten, and the Zani dismissed with a present of rice, and a hog or calf. Of the many ways in which the unhappy victim is destroyed, that just described is perhaps the least cruel, as in some places the flesh is cut off while the unfortunate creature is still alive."

This, then, was all that we knew in May, 1837, of the sacrifice of human beings among the Khond tribes of the hill tracts of Orissa, on the Madras side.

Mr. Ricketts, Commissioner at Cuttack, had sought for some information regarding this atrocious custom on the Bengal frontier, and received the following imperfect account. The Khonds supposed that good crops, and safety from all disease and accidents, were ensured by this slaughter. They considered it peculiarly necessary when engaged in the cultivation of turmeric. They very coolly reasoned as to the impossibility of the turmeric being of a fine deep colour without shedding of blood. They said they would not knowingly sacrifice a Khond or a Brahmin; with these two exceptions, victims of all ages and colours, of every religion and of both sexes, are equally acceptable, but the fat are considered more efficacious than the thin, and those in their prime than the aged and the young.

The victims are purchased at from sixty to one hundred and thirty rupees each, of persons of the Panu and Haree classes, who sell them as their own children; but as individuals of all classes are found amongst those rescued, it is evident that these miscreants steal them, and then sell them for slaughter to the Khonds.

The children, after being purchased, are often kept for many years. When of age to understand for what purpose they are intended, they are chained; two had been years in chains; one so long that he could not recollect ever having been at liberty. With the exception of being thus confined, they are well treated.

I was not successful in acquiring any reliable information as to the frequency of these sacrifices. One Khond, of about forty-six years of age, told me that he had witnessed fully fifty. Others equally old would acknowledge to having been present at two or three only. Victims are found in the houses of the village sirdars only, and mere ryots (labourers) are not permitted to slay victims—indeed, they have not the means, for a considerable expense falls on the master of the horrid feast.

Very contradictory stories were told of the manner in which the ceremony itself is conducted. The most common method appears to be, to bind the Meriah between two strong planks or bamboos, one being placed across the chest, another across the shoulders.

These are first of all firmly fastened at one end; the victim is then placed between them; a round is passed round the other ends, which are long enough to give a good purchase—they are brought together, and the unfortunate sufferer squeezed to death. While life is still ebbing, the body is thrown on the ground, and chopped in two pieces between the bamboos with hatchets.

Some accounts state that after the performance of several savage ceremonies and feastings, the divided corpse is buried unmutilated. Others say that, as soon as divided, each person in attendance falls on, and cuts a piece, which is carried away to be buried in his own land. Several admitted that in Goomsur the victims were cut up alive; and though no one would allow that to be the custom on this side (Bengal), I believe it is at least occasionally practised—for they acknowledge their belief that, if the body were buried whole, the benefit of the sacrifice would not extend farther than the lands of the person who found the victim; whereas, if more widely distributed, the benefit would be proportionally extended.

Such was the amount of our knowledge on this subject, which necessarily attracted the serious attention of both the governments of Madras and Bengal. What measures should be adopted, and what agency employed for the suppression of the horrible custom of human sacrifices, were questions frequently discussed. The dangers and difficulties attendant upon almost any plan were forcibly pointed out in the following report of Mr. Russell:—

"No one," he says, "is more anxious for the discontinuance of this barbarous practice than I am, but I am strongly impressed with the belief that it can be accomplished only by slow and gradual means. We must not allow the cruelty of the practice to blind us to the consequences of too rash a zeal in our endeavours to suppress it. The superstition of ages cannot be eradicated in a day; the people with whom we have to deal have become known to us only within the last few months, and our intercourse has been confined to a very small portion of a vast population, among the greater part of whom the same rites prevail, and of whose country and language we may be said to know almost nothing. Any measure of coercion would arouse the jealousy of a whole race, possessing the strongest feeling of clanship, and, whatever their ordinary dissensions, likely to make common cause in support of their common religion. The Bissois, the only people who could possibly be expected to second our views, have only a few peons in whom they could rely on such an occasion. The great mass of their subjects are Khonds; their influence is the moral effect of habit, not of physical power;

and men thus situated cannot be expected to aid in the compulsory abolition of a custom which all the surrounding tribes hold sacred. Are the Government prepared to engage in an undertaking which, to be effectual, must lead to the permanent occupation of an immense territory, and involve us in a war with people with whom we have now no connection, and no cause for quarrel, in a climate inimical to the constitution of strangers, and at an expense which no human foresight can calculate?

"From all I have seen of them, I feel convinced that no system of coercion can succeed. Our aim should be to improve to the utmost our intercourse with the tribes nearest to us, with a view to civilise and enlighten them, and so reclaim them from the savage practice, using our moral influence rather than our power. The position we now hold in Goomsur is favourable to the purpose, and it probably is so in some places beyond the frontier also."

It was finally resolved that I should be appointed, both in a revenue and magisterial capacity, to Goomsur, Sooradah, &c., with special charge over the Khond inhabitants of those countries. The experience I had gained during the war was likely to be most useful, and it was supposed that my information regarding the Khonds and their chiefs was superior to that of any one else who might have aspired to the same office.

I mention this the more particularly, as I have heard the propriety of the appointment called in question; but I think the testimony of Mr. Russell, recorded in a minute of consultation, should be conclusive, as he was the political agent during the two years' war, and in reality the only competent authority to decide on the subject. The minute is as follows:—

"Captain Campbell has acquired a knowledge of the country and people of the hill tracts in the Ganjam district, under circumstances never likely to occur again; and his local experience and personal influence with the different hill chieftains give him an advantage over any other person who could be appointed to the situation of principal assistant to the Commissioner.

CHAPTER V.

MY FIRST CRUSADE AGAINST THE MERIAH SACRIFICE—NATIVE CORPS RAISED BY MYSELF—GOOMSUR CHIEF—"BAHADUR BUKSHI," OTHERWISE SAM BISSOI—FIRST MEETING WITH THE KHOND LEADERS—A CONFERENCE—MY ADDRESS—A COMPROMISE SUGGESTED—REPLY OF THE ASSEMBLY—SURRENDER OF ONE HUNDRED INTENDED VICTIMS—OATH OF THE GOOMSUR CHIEFS—MY ADMINISTRATION OF JUSTICE AMONG THE KHONDS—MY FOUR YEARS' RESIDENCE AMONG THEM—BARGAINING AT FAIRS—CONSTRUCTION OF ROAD—SATISFACTORY RESULT OF MY FIRST CAMPAIGN—REGISTRATION OF SERFS.

CHAPTER V.

It was in the month of December, 1837, that I commenced my first crusade against Meriah sacrifice. The evil I had to combat had its root deep in the hearts of the Khonds; therefore, in the experiment I was about to make, it was imperative that I should act with the greatest moderation, and endeavour to persuade these mountain tribes peacefully to abandon a most horrible practice, which produced them no advantage, and, if persisted in, would expose them to the danger of a conflict with the British Government in India.

I was escorted on my trip by a few Sebundies, or irregular troops, raised and trained by myself for this special purpose; they were bold and hardy fellows, inhabiting the villages skirting the mountain range, and consequently well inured to the climate. From their youth upwards they were accustomed to bear arms, and were never so happy as when following the chase. Tigers and panthers they have often attacked single-handed, and the gallant deeds of their ancestors, as well as their own, had earned for them, from their rajahs, distinctive titles of honour. One, for instance, was called "The Lion of War" (Joogar Singh), another "Strong in Battle" (Runnah Singh), a third, "Swifter than a Lion" (Poki Singh), and so forth. A few of these men possessed a slight colloquial knowledge of the Khond dialect, which was of great use to me.

I also called to my aid the most influential chief of Upper Goomsur, a man of tried courage, whose services during the war had been invaluable. For these he had been nominated by the Government to the dignity of Chief of the Khonds of Goomsur, and the high title of "Babadur Bukshi" had been conferred upon him. I was intimate with this man, and felt confident that I could employ him as one of my most reliable instruments for effecting my purpose. We had been out on many a skirmish together during the campaign, and I had formed a high estimate of his character, which was shared by Mr. Russell. His name was Sam Bissoi.

With the shrewdness of character for which he was remarkable, he soon discovered that his real interests were bound up with those of the Government of the East India Company; hence his great services and devotion. This chief acted, as most men do, from motives of self-interest. Once satisfied on that point, his time and labour were most zealously and indefatigably given. During the war we shared many dangers in common, and I believe he entertained for me feelings of personal attachment.

I explained to him most fully my intended plan of procedure, and looked to him to prepare the minds of the Khonds for a free discussion of the question of human sacrifice, with a view to its abolition. Sam Bissoi, being a Hindoo, had no peculiar interest in maintaining this religious institution of the Khonds, although he was their chief. In truth, he cared very little about it one way or another. He certainly would never have moved a hand to abolish the rite at his own suggestion, but had not the least objection to help us to do so. Throughout my operations I can safely assert that I received from him the heartiest co-operation, and that he seconded my views most ably, and with all the power he could command. I never desired to place him in direct antagonism with his Khond tribes; indeed, I took good care (and so did he) that they should be well aware that he acted strictly and exclusively under my orders, and that, had he failed so to act, he would have been severely punished. In this position, as it were, of compulsion, he was better enabled to sway his wild followers, and to win them over to my views. He never ceased to urge upon them the necessity of obeying my orders, and attending to what I said.

I do not doubt that he professed to them in private his sorrow at thus being forced to take a part against their wishes; but as the war had not long terminated, and as the measures then adopted by Mr. Russell had been most rigorous, the old chief was able to illustrate and enforce his arguments by the terrible alternative of another display of the overwhelming power of the Anglo-Indian Government, should they obstinately refuse obedience on this important point.

Through Sam Bissoi, and another chief of some note, but far less intelligence, named Punda Naik, I summoned all the chiefs of the villages and districts (Mootahs) of the Goomsur hills to meet me in company with their Digaloos, or interpreters, at the little hill fort of Bodiagherry, where it may be remembered the Rajah sought refuge, and died during the war.

I need not say with what anxiety I anticipated this first meeting with my Khond clients and their leaders, on the all-important topic of the suppression of a ceremony so dearly cherished and so deeply venerated. It is true that I was generally known, and not disliked by the people, and it had fallen to my lot to invest the respective chiefs with the mark of their rank. It was merely a continuation of the ceremony their former masters, or rajahs, had practised, from which we saw no reason to depart—hence, at the conclusion of the war, each chief received from my hands the turban, or insignia of office; they consequently regarded me with favour, and I never lost an opportunity of strengthening the influence I had acquired.

At the appointed time nearly all the chiefs made their appearance at the spot named, accompanied by crowds of their Khond followers. There could not altogether have been less than three thousand at this first council. I received them all in a manner that I knew would be gratifying to them, and we then entered upon our conference.

I took my place under the shade of a tree, whilst the chiefs and many of their followers ranged themselves, squatted on the ground, in a semicircle in front; the rest of the Khonds, smoking vigorously, were collected in groups around us. These were chiefly the young men of the tribes, who rarely take part in the debates, having full confidence in and respect for their elders.

I made them a lengthened address through the medium of the two chiefs, Punda Naik and Sam Bissoi. I told them how painfully the English Government had been affected by the discovery of the horrible nature of the sacrifices they offered annually, in considerable numbers, to avert the wrath of the earth goddess. I said that the time had arrived when this savage and impious ceremony must terminate for ever. I was not there to upbraid them with the past, but to inaugurate for them a better future. I hoped that they did not desire to remain for ever in darkness, and allow all other tribes to outstrip them in the race of intelligence and civilization.

I assured them that a new era had dawned upon them. They were no longer subjects of an ignorant Rajah, who took no interest in their welfare and happiness, but by the fortune of war they had become the subjects of the British Government, in whose dominions the revolting ceremony I had come to denounce not only did not exist, but could not for a moment be tolerated. I told them that the British Government was a paternal one, and regarded all its subjects as its children, no matter of what caste or of what colour—there was and could be no distinction between Khond and Ooryah, and whenever the life of one was taken premeditatedly, no matter whether by sacrifice or otherwise, then assuredly would another life be required in punishment.

Was it not, I asked, their own rule?—head for head, life for life; was not this their universal law? And why should not this be applied to those whose lives they took away in sacrifice? Were these sacrifices really necessary? I asked them.

This I considered a most vital and important point, and I pressed it upon their consideration.

I thought it better to confess that we, like them, had once sacrificed human beings; like them, had indulged in similar cruel offerings; like them, had believed that the judgment of the gods could only be averted by a bloody expiation and the slaughter of our fellow-creatures; but this was in days of gross ignorance, when we were both fools and savages, knowing nothing, and living a debased and brutal life; but we emerged from this darkness, gradually obtained light, and at last gave up for ever our barbarous and unholy practices.

And what has been the consequence? I inquired. All kinds of prosperity have come upon us since we abolished those sinful rites; we now possess learning and wisdom, and see clearly the great folly we all committed. I told them that they must think of this, and be certain that their real welfare did not depend, as they falsely supposed, upon the continuance of this ceremony of their religion.

Putting aside ourselves, I continued, of whom they could not be expected to know much, I asked them to look at their neighbours on the plains; were not their crops as good and as abundant as those on the hills? Were not their cattle better? Were they not as well off as any hill tribe?

And do they sacrifice human beings? I demanded; yet nowhere can there be seen stronger men or finer crops.

I earnestly begged them to trust in my friendship, assuring them that there was nothing I would not willingly do to serve them. I reminded them that, as the representative of the British Government, I was empowered to speak with authority, and to promise, if they complied peacefully with what was now required, every favour it was in our power to grant. I entreated that they would bear in mind that I was not there to interfere with their religion; that I did not come amongst them to subvert their faith, but exclusively to prohibit a custom unsanctioned by the laws of God or man; my only wish being that they might abandon such wicked and cruel acts, and, under the protection of the Government whose subjects they now were, enjoy the fullest measure of prosperity, and live at peace amongst themselves and with their neighbours.

In short, I may say that I used every argument calculated to make an impression on such minds.

When I had finished my appeal, I requested that they would discuss the subject of it amongst themselves, and then communicate to me the result of their conference.

The assembly, which had listened patiently and calmly to all that had been said, then broke up. I awaited their return with much anxiety, as a compromise had been, if not exactly proposed, at least suggested to me, of allowing one sacrifice to take place annually, for the whole of the Khonds of Goomsur. This of course was immediately rejected.

The assembly again met, and after some preliminaries, five or six of the oldest and most influential of the Khond chiefs came forward to express the sentiments of the majority of the meeting, which they did with great self-possession and remarkable fluency, to the following purport :

"We have always sacrificed human beings. Our fathers handed down the custom to us. They thought no wrong, nor did we ; on the contrary, we felt we were doing what was right. We were then the subjects of the Rajah of Goomsur, now we are the subjects of the Great Government, whose orders we must obey. If the earth refuses its produce, or disease destroys us, it is not our fault ; we will abandon the sacrifice, and will, if permitted, like the inhabitants of the plains, sacrifice animals."

It would be tedious to relate all that passed, and the long and exciting discussions which ensued, but in the end the people were dismissed with orders to meet again on a certain day, bringing with them all the intended victims. The result was most gratifying, and far beyond my most sanguine hopes. At the appointed time, nearly one hundred human beings, male and female, intended for sacrifice, were delivered to me.

The assembly was again harangued by myself as on the first day, and subsequently addressed by several influential Khond speakers, who impressed upon its members the necessity of obedience to the orders of the State.

The chiefs then took an oath peculiar to themselves. Seated on tiger skins, they held in their hands a little earth, rice, and water, repeating as follows:

"May the earth refuse its produce, rice choke me, water drown me, and tiger devour me and my children, if I break the oath which I now take for myself and my people, to abstain for ever from the sacrifice of human beings."

My sword was then passed round from chief to chief, as a mark of submission on their part, and of protection on mine. Presents were distributed, after which I dissolved my second Khond Assembly, and all returned to their homes.

Some chiefs of the more distant villages had failed

to bring their Meriahs, but seeing how their fellow chieftains had acted, soon followed their example; thus one hundred and five were, in less than one month, rescued from a cruel death. They were of different ages. Many were restored to their relations on the plains; some were eagerly sought after for adoption by handicraftsmen, and others were taken to the low country. The civil and military officers took charge of a few, and I had twelve instructed as domestic servants, and to be employed as interpreters in our future intercourse with the Khonds.

I saw the Khonds daily and hourly; I went to their villages and ingratiated myself with them as much as possible. I spared no pains thoroughly to master the cases in which I had to adjudicate between them, and was invariably guided in my decisions by a council of their own elders; thus it may be said I administered their own laws, and in this way acquired considerable influence. I allowed no favourable opportunity to pass without a few words on the Meriah sacrifice; and as we gradually became more intimate, there was necessarily more freedom in the discussion.

In any altercations between tribes, I always supported the authority of their respective chiefs, and endeavoured in every way to conform myself to their usages and traditions, convinced that thus alone, in the first instance, could I effectively obtain their confidence, and through that confidence the important object of my mission.

I must remark that, although I did most sincerely desire to refrain from the exercise, as much as possible, of any other influence than that of persuasion over the minds and consciences of these wild and warlike races, yet that occasions more than once arose when it was necessary they should be reminded that I could use force, if unhappily the exercise of it became imperative. I was willing and most anxious on every other point to grant them all the concessions they desired, but on the one great question it was all-important that I should remain firm.

For four years I continued unceasingly to watch over them, visiting them in their mountain home once, and sometimes twice a year, during which visits I greatly strengthened the influence I had previously acquired. All matters which to them appeared important were then brought before me and settled. In all their most serious quarrels, not excluding blood feuds, I acted as their arbitrator; and was very frequently called upon to adjust their family disputes, in which I must say the weaker, as I may not call them *fair*, sex bore the most prominent part. I readily, and always with real pleasure, joined their hunting parties; and few, who have no experience of hill tribes, can estimate the vast amount of influence this simple act inspired.

I often received visits from them at my residence on the plains, as it was my wish they should mix freely with their lowland neighbours, as a means towards their civilization. Accordingly, I removed every impediment to their attending the fairs in the low country, and attracted as many as possible to visit them. In time they came in large numbers, and I took care at first that they should be protected against deceptions; but such precautions were soon found to be superfluous, for the mountaineers became expert bargainers, and were quite able to take care of themselves.

I instituted a strict search after kidnappers, and apprehended three notorious offenders, who were brought to trial and imprisoned.

I recommended the construction of a road through the heart of the Khond country, as the first great step towards the civilization of the inhabitants; and I urged, with all the force I could use, the necessity of extending operations for the suppression of the Meriah rite, into the neighbouring principalities of Boad and Chinna Kimedy.

My health had suffered much from personal exposure in these unhealthy regions, where a tree or a straw heap was very frequently my only shelter at night. Though such make-shifts are not to be com plained of when on service in the field, they are far from agreeable in the ordinary routine of a peaceful duty; but I was well repaid by the peace and repose which prevailed in the countries under my charge, and by the fact that in January, 1842, the Meriah sacrifice was at an end among the Khonds of Goomsur, though I did not pretend to have eradicated all inclination for the rite from the minds of these wild people.

Thus terminated what I may designate as my first campaign, with the special object of conquering the religious prejudices of the wild tribes of Goomsur, and extinguishing their atrocious rite of sacrificing human victims.

I desire in all sincerity to speak with diffidence of my own exertions, and regret the necessity of such frequent and unavoidable use of the personal pronoun. But I may be allowed warmly to rejoice over the results of these five years of labour. The chieftains and their tribes were my attached friends. A commencement of civilization had been made, more than one hundred victims saved from a violent and bloody death, and the public performance of the Meriah sacrifice entirely suppressed amongst the Hill Tribes of Goomsur.

In addition to this, I had carefully registered all the Possiapoes, or serfs, who were in the hands of the Khonds. These serfs are well-treated, and in no immediate danger; but as there is always a remote probability of their sacrifice, I considered it a wise measure of precaution to see them all, inscribe their names, ages, &c., in a list kept for that purpose, and then restore them to their owners only on the security of the most influential and noteworthy chiefs; and on the express condition of being presented to me, or to whoever I might at any time depute to represent me, when I wished to see them.

CHAPTER VI.

I AM ORDERED FOR SERVICE IN CHINA—MR. BANNERMAN'S COMMENDATION OF MY PROCEEDINGS—CAPTAIN M'PHERSON APPOINTED MY SUCCESSOR—IS PREJUDICED AGAINST SAM BISSOI—REPORT OF MR. SMOLLETT THE COMMISSIONER—INCREASED POWERS CONFERRED ON THE AGENT —REVOLT OF GOOMSUR—OPPRESSION OF THE NATIVE ASSISTANTS EMPLOYED IN THE AGENCY—DESCENT OF ARMED KHONDS INTO THE LOW COUNTRY—MY RETURN TO MY FORMER POST—I RECALL SAM BISSOI—TAKE THE COMMAND OF A FORCE AGAINST THE RAJAH OF NUGOOL—FLIGHT OF THE RAJAH—HIS PURSUIT AND CAPTURE—DESCRIPTION OF THE COUNTRY.

CHAPTER VI.

EARLY in the year 1842, the regiment to which I belonged was ordered on service to China. I applied, through my immediate superior, Mr. Bannerman, then Commissioner in Ganjam, for permission to join my corps prior to its embarkation for foreign service. Mr. Bannerman, in forwarding my application to the Madras Government, was pleased to observe—"In submitting this communication, it may be permitted me to express my acknowledgment of the very valuable assistance I have received from Major Campbell during the last four years; and my regret should the exigencies of the public affairs in other quarters cause the temporary withdrawal of his service from this district."

I accordingly quitted Goomsur, and had the opportunity of visiting one of the most interesting countries in the world. But as this book does not profess to treat of China, I will merely observe that I remained there until the war was over, and indeed for some twelve months after; and that, in recognition of my services, I was so fortunate as to get a step in promotion, and to receive admission into the Order of the Bath.

Captain McPherson took my place amongst the Khonds. This officer had some time previously proceeded into the Khond country of Souradah, where female infanticide prevailed. He was accompanied by troops, and provided with elephants to carry his tents; but a few days—about twenty-five—sufficed to disorganise the whole party, who were driven back to the plains, and entirely prostrated by fever, which prevails to an extraordinary extent throughout the hills.

In 1843 and 1844 he passed a brief period, twenty or five and twenty days in the Goomsur Khond country, but did not penetrate into the interior, nor indeed was it necessary, so long as he intended to confine his operations to Goomsur; for the Khonds, as I have stated in the previous chapter, had relinquished sacrifice, though they clamoured loudly (as they had done when I left them), at the glaring injustice of our tolerating the rite in the adjacent countries of Boad and Chinna Kimedy, whilst it was not permitted amongst them. In these provinces the Meriah sacrifice was openly performed, and in several instances the flesh of the victim was brought from thence to their fields by the Khonds of Goomsur. This was a sore trial to such as were sincerely desirous of adhering to their pledge.

Captain McPherson conceived a strong prejudice against the man who had rendered the best services to the Anglo-Indian Government; first to Mr. Russell, during the rebellion, and subsequently to myself, in inducing his tribes to forego the rite I desired to abolish. Apparently this officer had been persuaded by his native subordinates, in whom he seems to have placed too much reliance, that Sam Bissoi was fomenting intrigues in Khondistan, and that his summary removal was imperative. The result was, that the Government was induced to sanction the deposition and banishment of this most deserving chief, and of several of the members of his family. From that hour, and a most evil one it was, there was no peace in Goomsur.

In place of Sam Bissoi, a priest of Tentilghur, named Ootan Singh, was set up; and Captain McPherson reported that this measure, namely, the substitution of Ootan Singh for Sam Bissoi, had "shed light and repose on the distracted minds of the Khonds." But the very reverse of this was the fact, as the reader will soon see.

Shortly after the banishment of Sam Bissoi, Captain McPherson went to Calcutta, and was succeeded, *pro tempore*, by Dr. Cadenhead, a most able and talented officer. The following is an extract from the report of Mr. Smollett, through whom, as Commissioner, it was necessary the Doctor should make his communications to Government. It is dated September, 1845:—

"In July, 1844, Captain McPherson proceeded to Bengal, on leave, and has not yet returned. His place was occupied by Mr. Assistant-Surgeon Cadenhead, who took the Khond Agency on the same independent footing that his predecessor enjoyed. Mr. Cadenhead's reports of his visit to the hills have recently been before Government. Of these it need only be said that, on visiting the Hodzoghoro Mootah, he found the Dulbehra, Ootan Singh, insulted and derided, without authority or power, and deprived of his lands. The Khonds, said to have been delighted to escape from Sam Bissoi's tyranny and oppression, were again banded together under one of his relations, previously held too insignificant for removal, and all expressed their determination to revert to sacrifice. The tribes, however, yielded to Mr. Cadenhead's remonstrances till his back was turned, when they again rebelled, and the Bara and Atarah Mutah Khonds following in the train, announced their intention of returning to their superstitions, unless the people of Boad were coerced with themselves."

The above is sufficient to show that a fatal mistake had been committed in deposing Sam Bissoi. I trace much of the mischief which afterwards occurred in the Boad country to this cause. It inspired the resolute with a spirit of opposition, and the timid fled into concealment. Even Captain McPherson was dissatisfied with the new chief whom he had appointed, and stated, in one of his reports to Government, that this man, Ootan Singh, had so disgusted the people by his avarice, his want of courage, and his bad faith, that he was compelled to contemplate his removal.

Such was the condition of the Khond Hills of Goomsur in 1845, towards the end of which year the supreme Government determined to remodel the agency for the suppression of human sacrifices, and to confer upon the agent and his assistants extensive powers. Captain McPherson was named agent, and early in 1846 took the field in the Boad country. It adjoins Goomsur, but is in Bengal territory.

He states that he found the Boad tribes more prepared than he had ventured to hope to adopt the required changes. Every tribe was pledged by its representatives, after the manner of the Goomsur tribes, to relinquish the Meriah rite ; and as the possessors of victims continued to bring them with emulous haste, in seven days about one hundred and seventy were delivered to him.

This was certainly a bright beginning, and seemed to be ripe with promise for the new agency, from which so much had been expected. Alas, a disastrous reverse was near at hand, for within one week of the delivery of these victims to the agent of the Government, his camp was surrounded by an armed mob of Khonds, who demanded and unhappily obtained their restoration.

I feel assured that the agent was both misled and misinformed by his native subordinates, when he consented to surrender these poor victims to their barbarous masters. He states himself that "it was the Rajah of Boad who prayed earnestly that he might have an opportunity of bringing the Khonds back to a right state of mind; also, that he, the Rajah, undertook to effect this, and would give a solemn guarantee for their safety and redelivery, if I would make over the victims to him."

This Rajah was a poor imbecile youth, utterly incapable of influencing Khonds or others for good or evil. His guarantee, if ever given, which he himself stoutly denied, was entirely worthless. Of this the agent soon had ample proof; for scarcely had this first concession of the surrender of the victims been made, when, flushed with such a success, the Khonds again attacked his camp, which was then retiring on Goomsur. They now demanded that this imbecile

Rajah, who was then accompanying Captain McPherson—and whom the Khonds supposed to be a prisoner—should be made over to them. To pacify them, a second concession was made, and the Rajah was sent back with them to Boad.

I have no wish to dwell upon these deplorable mistakes of judgment, nor to bring odium upon any one responsible for them; but I must say that I have not the faintest doubt that this rapid transition of the Khonds from a spirit of confidence and obedience, as evinced by the delivery of their victims, to one of distrust and revolt, accompanied by demands not unlike threats, was caused exclusively by the exactions and oppressions to which they had been subjected by the native assistants of Captain McPherson. Money was extorted from them, cooking utensils were forcibly carried away, and even the Rajah himself was mulcted of a pair of gold armlets.

This lamentable state of affairs was necessarily continued in consequence of the rainy season having compelled the withdrawal to the low country of the agent and his camp. It was hoped that when operations could be renewed he would recover both the prestige he had lost, and the intended victims again in the hands of the exasperatod Khonds.

But the plot thickened; and, in addition to the disastrous state of things on the hills, a new revolution broke out, at the head of which was a man named Chokro Bissoi, nephew of the former chief of the Goomsur Khonds, and, as subseqnent events proved, a very clever and skilful leader. He had been living in the neighbouring principality of Ungool, but came from his retirement in this emergency, in the hope of replacing his uncle in power.

Revolt was general in both Goomsur and Boad; it had spread so extensively, that when the cessation of the rains permitted Captain McPherson to march with the force at his command into Boad, he found nothing but deserted villages—the people having fled to the recesses of their jungles, conveying thither all their grain and valuables. Their villages were frequently burnt, and the dense jungles searched by the troops; but on several occasions they met with a sharp resistance from the Khonds, who made no signs of submission, although all their principal places were in military possession of the troops.

Unfavourable as was this position for the agent, it was aggravated by the descent of Chokro Bissoi to the low country, a manœuvre which he devised, and, with a band of followers, skilfully executed. Once on the plains, he commenced burning and plundering in every direction, apparently in retaliation of what had been done in Boad by the Captain's detachment.

This critical state of affairs alarmed the supreme

Government; and they requested the authorities at Madras to depute an experienced general officer, with a sufficient force, to proceed to Goomsur and quell the disturbances. In accordance with this suggestion, General Dyce was named to the command. He quickly marched into the disturbed district, and, through his judicious measures, tranquillity was so far restored as to render it possible again to renew operations against human sacrifices, which, from first to last, had been the sole object the Anglo-Indian Government had in view.

The chief rebel, Chokro Bissoi was still at large, and roaming about Boad with a few followers, a nucleus of mischief, apparently, that it required careful observation and a cautious policy to render innocuous.

While these troublous events were occurring, I had returned from China, and been employed in suppressing an insurrection at Golcondah, which was quickly put down. Very soon after this, I was informed by the Marquis of Tweeddale, the Governor and Commander-in-chief of the Madras Presidency, that I should probably be required to return to my old work in Goomsur. I mention this fact, which occurred in January, 1847, to prove that it is not true, as so often stated, that Captain McPherson was removed from office in consequence of General Dyce's reports. The intention of the Bengal Government was confirmed no doubt by those reports, but that intention existed before the General had written a line on the subject.

When about to return to the scene of my old labours, I took upon myself the grave responsibility of recalling from exile the chief, Sam Bissoi, well knowing that his re-appearance in Khondistan would have the best effect upon the tribes generally, and tend powerfully to allay the excitement caused by the late disturbances. He ascended the Ghauts along with me, and it was affecting to see the reverence with which the people received their old Abba, as they called him, as he passed them on his way to his paternal property of Hodghogur.

I have never had reason to regret this healing measure, of which I took upon myself the entire responsibility. I believe it was an act of justice to a meritorious and useful man, whose previous good service to Government had deserved a better recompense than disgrace and banishment. The Governor-General eventually confirmed what I had done; and thus my old and valued ally once more became the chief of a portion of the Khond tribes. He well knew how to govern these people, and how to make himself both feared and respected. His will emphatically was law, and in no part of the land were the tribes better cared for or more prosperous than in the little dominion subject to his rule. His manner of presenting his tribes was, for a man with his educational deficiences, most remarkable. He marshalled them always at a little distance from my tents, and then having arranged them in their order of precedence, he led them successively into my presence, in a most graceful and courtly manner. No Lord Chamberlain could have performed the office better.

I now found the Goomsur tribes in a feverish state, consequent upon the marching and countermarching of troops through their country, and their ignorance of what the Government intended to do. It was my duty to re-assure them, and to restore the confidence which the late measures had weakened or destroyed. Having formerly passed many years with these tribes, I had not much difficulty in bringing them to reason. I learnt with unfeigned pleasure that no public performance of the Meriah rite had taken place since I had left them, and I could not discover that there had been any private one. I believe they had remained faithful to their pledge, and I marked my approval of their steadfastness by the bestowal amongst them of several yards of a coarse red cloth which I knew they most highly prized.

We talked over the old question of the prohibited rite. They did not suffer, they said, from its abolition amongst them, but at times they became impatient of restraint when they heard of sacrifices in Boad, Jeypore, and other neighbouring states. They hoped the Government would act impartially, and exact from others the same obedience it had required and received from them.

This I readily promised should be done; and after adjudicating in all the disputed cases brought before me, I took leave of my Goomsur Khonds. Then I crossed over into the Boad country, where peace had not been perfectly restored, and the surrendered victims still remained in the hands of the wild tribes of the district.

The great feat to be achieved here was to get back the one hundred and seventy victims, and to restore confidence to the Khonds. After late events they entertained a great dread of the visit of any agent of Government; having met with unmerciful treatment at the hands of the native employés, they had retaliated so sharply that they feared severe punishment. Consequently they fled to their forests on my approach, and I could find no one to treat with.

In this dilemma I was preparing to carry into effect such measures as I thought advisable to effect a reconciliation between the Khonds and the Government, when I was somewhat suddenly ordered to take the military and political control of an expedition destined to depose the Rajah of the neighbouring principality of Ungool.

The Government of India had resolved on this severe measure in consequence of the Rajah's continued insubordination and disobedience to their commands. I may state that in a semi-official letter to the President of the Council of India, I had, two months previously, pleaded as urgently as possible the Rajah's cause, and said what I could in palliation of his conduct. The supreme authority felt, I presume, that resistance to their authority and commands was not to be tolerated on the part of this petty ruler, as the example might be contagious, and there were some twenty or twenty-five so called independent Rajahs in the same neighbourhood. An ultimatum was accordingly prepared and forwarded to the Rajah, intimating that if in twenty-five days its conditions were not fulfilled, he would be considered as deposed, and his country taken from him. Of course it was never supposed he would comply with the terms of this ultimatum, and I therefore descended the hills to place myself at the head of the troops destined to act against this refractory chief.

The force at my disposal consisted of two complete regiments of Madras Native Infantry, the 41st and 29th, with some companies of the 22nd, and the full complement of Artillery. Colonel Ouseley, the

Governor-General's Agent for the South West Frontier, was ordered to co-operate with me, and to place at my disposal any portion of the cavalry or infantry of the Ramghur contingent that I might desire. No one knew anything of the country against which we were about to proceed. It was said to be studded with forts well mantled with guns, and to support a standing army of seventeen thousand soldiers. I put very little trust in these rumours, and felt very confident that my small army would give a good account of the enemy, wherever met or however strongly posted. I must not omit to mention that I took with me, from Goomsur, a small body of my faithful irregulars, or Sebundies, and found them literally invaluable.

Early in January we marched from Berhampore, in Ganjam, and arrived on the borders of the Ungool country on the 20th of January. I had issued the most stringent orders that no plundering or marauding, the vice of native troops, should be permitted; and I took care that the inhabitants of the country we passed through should receive the full value of whatever they sold. Still great fear was often displayed by the people, rumour having magnified my little army into a force twenty times its number. I had not more than two thousand fighting men, and four guns, and to my great surprise I marched this force into the Rajah's country without meeting the slightest resistance. It is true I came upon a wretched bamboo stockade near Huttui, on the borders of Ungool, but it was not defended.

Once in Ungool, I necessarily sought the most trustworthy information regarding the Rajah, his residences and forts, and the best means of approaching them. The result I will now relate.

The Rajah, it was said, resided at the foot of a hill, in the most inaccessible part of his country; his dwelling was not fortified, but defended by two stockades, erected on two hills that commanded the main road leading to it. The works were reported strong, and guns would be requisite to reduce them. In addition to these stockades, there was a small fort erected on an eminence at Tikripurrah, and a new fortification, consisting of a gate with strong stockades, had recently been built near the Rajah's residence. There was also a new gate and stockade at a place called Borokheta.

It seemed, then, that at last we were likely to meet some determined resistance. I resolved to open the campaign by an attack on the fort at Tikripurrah. Thither we groped our way with all due precaution, till we came in view of this hill fort, which was said to be defended by two thousand men. Its situation was well chosen, on the top of a long narrow hill, with a commanding range on the small plain below, over which any attacking force must march.

The guns were soon loaded and in position, and I advanced with a portion of the 41st regiment up the face of the hill to the centre of the fort. The enemy appeared taken by surprise, and offered no resistance; they fled in a crowd, exchanged a few shots in their flight with our troops, but there was no "butcher's bill," not so much as a casualty on either side.

I found this fortification tolerably constructed, and had it been resolutely defended, the place might have cost me much trouble to take. A strong wooden wall ran round it, and the interior was well fitted up. There were a few guns, and a large quantity of almost useless powder. I ordered the entire demolition of this fort, and then marched onwards towards the Rajah's own residence.

To condense as much as possible, I may say that in our advance the only impediments we had to encounter were those placed in our way by Nature; and that, when we reached the Rajah's dwelling, we found it as deserted as the stockades, or fortifications, that had been placed on the main road for its defence. The villages were all empty, and the Rajah was said to have hidden himself in the dense forests, and to be attended in his flight by some of his seraglio, and by his commander-in-chief, named Sindu Ghur Naik.

I took all the guns, matchlocks, gunpowder, saltpetre, sulphur, and lead that were in the Ungool arsenal. Altogether I think I captured nine or ten guns of different sizes.

It only now remained to hunt out the Rajah and his followers, and for this purpose I divided my force as judiciously as I could, and posted detachments in positions where they were likely to be of most service in arresting the fugitives. This important object was attained chiefly through the zeal of the retainers of a friendly and neighbouring chief, aided by my own irregulars, who got upon the scent of the Rajah, and caught him when he was literally being carried away in the arms of some of his women. He could not help himself, for he is a cripple; so he succumbed to the overpowering force of circumstances, and was brought a prisoner into my camp.

His name was Somnath Singh, and he differed in no wise from his brother potentates, whom I have already described. He was not an old man in years, but a complete wreck from the combined effects of dissipation and rheumatism.

A few days after the capture of this man, his chief advisers were cleverly caught in a large hole they had dug in the thick forest, where they hoped to elude detection. They were surrounded by a body of my irregulars, who advanced upon them, gradually narrowing the circle, until they were able to seize and pinion them without any mischief being done. Sindu Ghur Naik was undoubtedly the moving spirit in Ungool, where he bore a bad reputation, and instigated his master to the course which ended in their common ruin.

In less than six weeks from leaving Berhampore, the mission entrusted to me by the Governor-General was fully and perfectly achieved; all the little forts were dismantled, the guns in our possession, the Rajah and his principal men captured, and the people had returned to their villages.

I had no power to do anything with the deposed Rajah, or his chief servants, save to forward them as close prisoners of war to Cuttack, there to be dealt with as the Government might please. I did so, and I can now add that the Rajah remained a prisoner on parole for a few years at Cuttack, and died; and that most of his followers were shot down by a company of Sepoys while making an attempt to escape from prison.

I received the thanks of Lord Hardinge for this service, and was at liberty to turn my attention to Boad and the sacrificing tribes.

Before finally quitting Ungool, let me say that I do not think its annexation to the British dominions any very valuable acquisition. It is a small principality, in the centre of a cluster of little independent states, and is separated from the Boad country by the noble Mahanuddy river. It is hilly generally, with thick forests, producing that valuable tree, the saal, from which gun carriages are made, superior to any I have seen. No natural obstacles are insurmountable, as we had proof during this campaign, by carriages built of this timber. Iron is also found in considerable abundance, and the different grains common to these hill tracts grow in the cultivated districts. There are a few valleys, fertile enough; but the jungle fever, which is very fatal, is seldom absent from this land, and no European constitution could endure a prolonged residence here. The rite of human sacrifice, if it ever obtained in these hills, has long ceased, and animals only are slaughtered.

Of Boad as well as Goomsur, my Assistant, Captain Macviccar, had been placed in charge during my absence, with directions to abstain, if possible, from all aggressive movements, yet to keep the disaffected in check. This he was enabled to do, and also to prevent the consummation of an intended sacrifice.

A young girl had gone through all the preliminary ceremonies; she had been shewn to and accepted by the deity, and the day for immolation had been appointed. Intelligence of this reached Captain Macviccar, who did not lose a moment in sending aid to the intended victim, by which means she was rescued from a cruel death. Four of the Khond chiefs concerned in this outrage were captured, and remained as prisoners in camp until my arrival from Ungool.

CHAPTER VII.

INTRIGUES OF A KHOND CHIEF IN BOAD—MEASURES TAKEN THERE BY ME, ASSISTED BY CAPTAIN MACVICCAR, TO SUPPRESS HUMAN SACRIFICE—DISCUSSIONS WITH THE LEADERS—COMPARISON OF NEW ZEALAND SAVAGE AND KHOND—THE YOUNG WARRIORS—MY PROLONGED SOJOURN IN BOAD—EFFECTS OF THE UNHEALTHY CLIMATE—THE CHIEFS PLEDGED NOT TO PERMIT HUMAN SACRIFICE—RESCUE OF TWO HUNDRED AND THIRTY-FIVE INTENDED VICTIMS—CEREMONIES DURING A SACRIFICE—I QUIT BOAD.

CHAPTER VII.

AFTER the termination of my campaign in Ungool, I proceeded to Boad, taking with me six companies of infantry and a troop of irregular horse. Captain Macviccar had been enabled to preserve tranquillity in this country, notwithstanding the attempts made by the rebel leader, Chokro Bissoi, to compromise the Khonds by some overt act of hostility towards us. The latter was prodigal of his promises if they would only join him in resisting the Government; they might then, he assured them, sacrifice human victims whenever they pleased, without let or hindrance. Such a promise was precisely adapted to gain the devotion of the Khonds, and as they still possessed the destined victims extorted from the late agent, it cannot surprise any one if their position should be considered exceedingly critical.

The people hesitated. They entertained a wholesome dread of the power of the Sirkar, or Government. During my absence in Ungool there had been no attack on Captain Macviccar's camp; indeed, he had been able to conciliate a few chiefs, and was thus afforded some means of communicating with the great body of the mountaineers and their leaders, who still held aloof from temptation.

We were now on the eve of deciding the great question, whether the Supreme Government in India could or could not enforce its will, and effectually suppress the sacrifice of human beings in Boad?

Our success in Goomsur was a powerful means of co-operation; for there was positive proof that the deity could not require human blood, as uninterrupted prosperity attended on those tribes that had long ceased to offer it. The war in Ungool was likewise not without its effect. The tribes said, cunningly enough, if Chokro Bissoi could not keep his friend, the Rajah of Ungool, on his throne, how can he secure us the privileges he promises?

I commenced my work in Boad by a careful distribution of the small force at my disposal, taking good care that private property should be scrupulously respected, and, whenever opportunity offered, I treated the inhabitants of these hill valleys with the greatest kindness and consideration. Captain Macviccar pursued the same policy, and was within two days' march of me with an adequate force, using his best endeavours to persuade the people that our mission amongst them was friendly and peaceful. I sent emissaries in every direction. Gradually, to my great satisfaction, the deserted villages began to be reoccupied, and as the advanced guard of the population were not only left unmolested, but treated with kindness, the great mass of the people soon followed.

In about six weeks the chieftains were prepared to enter on the discussion of the real subject of our coming amongst them.

I was always accessible to the Khonds and their leaders, and thought no time ill spent in arguing with them about their much-loved rite. We had council after council; at all hours and in various places; sometimes in my tent, but more generally in the open forest. Often my patience was terribly tested, for after an objection had been started, discussed, and I hoped finally disposed of, some stupid chief would raise precisely the same point again, and then we had to travel over the old ground and repeat all the old arguments.

It not unfrequently happened that in these Khond Parliaments several of the leading members were in a state of intoxication; if they became boisterous, which seldom happened, their brother chiefs led them away; but most commonly they sat quietly enough, smoking and shaking their heads very gravely, as if they understood all that was going on.

For days and weeks these councils continued; and it was evident that we were fast gaining ground upon the native prejudices. I never omitted an opportunity of using any suitable argument to wean them from their detestable practice. I met with much evasion and much falsehood; and many intrigues and stratagems were resorted to to baffle my efforts.

I have somewhere read that the Khonds were "a clear-minded and truthful people," but from whom they could have inherited these rare qualities is to me incomprehensible. I found them just what I expected barbarians to be—sunk in the depths of ignorance, superstition, and sensuality. Between the New Zealand savage, who regales himself on human flesh, and the Hill Khond of Orissa, who pitilessly immolates a human victim, there was nothing to prefer; the one had not outstripped the other in civilization, nor had either (except in a few favoured spots) yet had the opportunity of emerging from utter barbarism. The Khonds are probably not quite so expert at a lie as their more civilized neighbours of the plains; but regard for truth, for its own sake, they have none—absolutely none whatever. Like all savages, and, I might add, all Orientals, they require to be dealt with much more of the *fortiter in re* than the *suaviter in modo*. The utmost amount of persuasion and conciliation is not inconsistent with firmness and resolution.

It need surprise no one, then, to learn that I was successful, and met with the greatest attention, when, in the most plain, straightforward, and forcible language, I assured them of the resolution of the Government—by persuasion, if possible—but in any event to put down this most inhuman practice. If a chief, as happened once or twice, was very refractory, and would listen to no reason, I found out his quarters and quietly surrounded his village with troops. This kind of argument was quite irresistible; there were no means of escape, and as after all no harm was done, we speedily became good friends again. This simple demonstration of physical force was sufficient to overcome his scruples; and necessity, a stronger influence than antipathy, converted an enemy into an ally.

Thus it was imperative at times to threaten, and at times to coax them into submission. I went daily to their villages, and the trivial act of taking a light for my cigar from the first Khond at hand, gained me many friends. In fact, I omitted no opportunity of proving how sincerely I desired their welfare, and would forward it on the sole condition of the discontinuance of human sacrifices.

It would be tedious to dwell upon my debates

with the Khonds. I generally found a minority of hot-blooded youths, who were always for resistance and war; but when once I had won over the chiefs and elders of the several tribes, I knew there was nothing to fear from these impetuous young warriors. All important points amongst the Khonds are decided by the elders of the tribes, and from their decision there is no appeal.

I visited every nook and corner of Boad, and some most frightful regions, reeking with fever, and quite uninhabitable by Europeans, were traversed, but not without my camp severely suffering. Still it was of the last importance that the work in Boad, where the Government had been checked and defeated, should now be thoroughly accomplished; that every tribe should feel that they were accessible, and could not be hidden from us; above all, that we should satisfy those chiefs who first made their submission, and swore to renounce human sacrifice, that what had been exacted from them would be rigidly exacted from all. We had promised them this, cost what it might; it was necessary that they should see how faithfully we kept our promise.

I remained, therefore, in Boad until May, an unusually late period, and most unhealthy. To add to our comforts at this season of the year, the rank grass and underwood in the jungles are set fire to, in anticipation of the rains in June; and it may readily be imagined that the combined effects of the sun's rays and the dense hot smoke of the burning forests, rendered the Boad hills anything but a paradise. Fever abounded in camp, and I was obliged to send numbers of men to the low country to recruit their health. Two officers, I grieve to say, died, and others had to seek in distant lands a renovation of life.

Yet, with all these heavy drawbacks, our success was very great, and as I saw the chiefs of every tribe gradually wavering, and ultimately yielding to our determination to succeed, I felt that now or never was the decisive moment with the Khonds of Boad.

Every chief successively swore to abstain henceforth from offering human victims; all pledged themselves with the formalities most binding amongst their tribes; they swore upon a tiger skin, performed unmeaning ceremonies, and vowed in the most solemn manner that they would keep their pledge.

As a tangible proof of their sincerity, they delivered up every Meriah in their possession. Three of the victims, out of the one hundred and seventy formerly surrendered, had been cruelly slaughtered, in the vain hope of propitiating their deity, and preventing the success of our efforts. With these exceptions I got back all who had been redelivered—the total number rescued in Boad during these operations being two hundred and thirty-five. All these became at once wards of the Government, and their future welfare was in our hands. How we performed our task I will presently state.

When it is remembered with what care these victims are fed, fostered, and cherished until the hour of sacrifice arrives, even at that supreme moment being regarded as something more than mortal, it will hardly surprise any one to learn that, so far from being grateful to us for saving them from a cruel death, the majority appeared almost indifferent, and many betrayed great fear when told they were to go with us to the plains, as they knew not what lot awaited them there. Nothing else could have been expected from a class so ignorant; it only, however, required a very short time to reconcile them all to their new position, and to awaken a slight feeling of gratitude for the deliverance effected.

I will here briefly describe one mode in which the sacrifice is performed in Boad.

Three days previous to immolation there is great feasting, rioting, and dancing, and the most gross and brutal licentiousness. On the fourth day the Meriah is taken round the village in procession to each door, when some pluck hair from his head, and others solicit a drop of his saliva, with which they anoint their own heads. Afterwards the victim is drugged, and then taken to the place of sacrifice, his head and neck being introduced into the reft of a strong bamboo split in two, the ends of which are secured and held by the sacrificers. The presiding priest then advances, and with an axe breaks the joints of the legs and arms; after which the surrounding mob strip off the flesh from the bones with their knives, and each man, having secured a piece, carries the quivering and bloody morsel to his fields, and there buries it.

It was now full time to quit the hills and return to the low country. I was enabled to report to the Government the restoration of order and tranquillity in these hills. The rebel, Chokro Bissoi, had been fairly hunted out, bitterly upbraiding the Khonds with having deserted him.

I took a friendly leave of the hill chiefs, exhorting them to stand fast to their pledge, and to expect me again amongst them in a few months; meantime I assured them that I should always see them with pleasure on the plains, and gladly be their friend and counsellor to settle their intertribal feuds. I gave presents of beads to their wives and children. Thus terminated most successfully our first campaign in Boad.

This success, and the rescue of so many victims, amply recompensed us for all the privations and sufferings we had to endure both day and night. I say night, because our sleep was too frequently disturbed by the hideous shrieks of the hyenas which abound in those hills, and the somewhat softer roar of the panthers. In the more unfrequented parts of the mountains this concert was enlivened by the unmelodious yelling of packs of wild dogs, attracted to our camp by the little flock of sheep or goats which we were obliged to take with us for food. These precious herds, which kept us from starving, were jealously guarded, and every precaution taken to prevent their furnishing a stray panther with a supper, but, notwithstanding all our care, several were carried off.

One of my irregular guard possessed a fighting ram, which was a prime favourite both with his master and with all in camp. This ram, for safety, slept in the little tent which served as a shelter to his owner and several other men. Early one morning all were startled out of their sleep by a noise, as of a struggle, and jumping up, they beheld their favourite in the act of being carried off by a panther. In a moment they were in pursuit, and their shouts and cries caused the retreating brute to drop his prey in a small thicket on the outskirts of the camp. The body of the unfortunate ram was found cruelly lacerated, and his sorrowing owner and friends had no consolation left but to divide the remains, and—

the unpoetic truth must be told—eat them, for meat was very scarce in camp. A solemn vow of vengeance was registered against the panther, and executed in the following manner.

It was as certain as anything could be that at dusk the panther would return to the thicket to seek his abandoned prey; accordingly the ram's skin was stuffed with grass, and placed almost in the very spot where the panther had dropped him in the morning. Close at hand was an unerring shot, a trusty friend of the late ram's owner, and a very brave fellow withal.

Just at sunset, the panther was sighted on the border of the jungle, apparently meditating his best line of approach, which, having settled, he crept with stealthy cat-like pace till within a few yards of the decoy; then sprang upon it with a tremendous bound. With a low growl of satisfaction, he was preparing to carry off his prey, when the hunter's bullet sped true to the aim, and the ram was avenged! The dead panther was carried in triumph to the camp, but his well-deserved fate had not the least effect in deterring others from helping themselves, as often as opportunity occurred, to our sheep and goats.

The rainy season was passed in the low country recruiting our health, and gathering information for our intended crusade next season against human sacrifices in Chinna Kimedy.

CHAPTER VIII.

DESCRIPTION OF CHINNA KIMEDY—SUPERSTITIOUS PRACTICES THERE—I PROPOSE A PLAN OF OPERATIONS—BY A HASTY MARCH I PREVENT A GENERAL SACRIFICE—CONCILIATE THE RAJAHS—CONDITION OF THESE MOUNTAINEERS—ELEPHANT IDOLS OVERTHROWN—RECOVERY OF TWO HUNDRED AND SIX INTENDED VICTIMS—SUCCESSFUL RESULTS OF THE MISSION—NEW ROAD IN PROGRESS—THE KHOND LANGUAGE—EFFECTS OF FEVER—AM ORDERED TO THE CAPE.

CHAPTER VIII.

Chinna Kimedy is a principality a little to the south and west of Goomsur, having about one hundred and twenty villages on the plains, which are fertile. The inhabitants are for the most part Ooryahs, who have frequently suffered from the incursions of the adjoining mountaineers (Khonds), whose savage valour generally obtained for them an easy victory—while, in case of a reverse, their fastnesses received them, and their impenetrable jungles afforded a secure retreat.

The late Rajah was accused of tyrannical conduct by the Khond tribes who professed allegiance to him, and they invaded and devastated the low country, carrying the Rajah and his three sons captives to their mountains. After some time, the old man was ransomed for a considerable sum, and his son, the present Rajah, released, because he was supposed to be at enmity with his father. From this it will be apparent that the low country Rajahs are most unwilling to risk a collision with the hill tribes, which was an important fact to be borne in mind in our attempts to suppress human sacrifice. There must necessarily be a good understanding between the chiefs and us, but I could not sanction any proceeding tending to excite animosity in the Khonds against their Rajahs, for being aiders and abettors in our plans to extirpate their long-cherished rite.

The Khond Maliahs of Chinna Kimedy comprise a portion of the chain of mountains in continuation of those of Boad and Goomsur, both of which it adjoins. The inhabitants are essentially of the same stock, and their tribal divisions very similar. The Khond chiefs of villages and Mootas are termed Maji, instead of Mulliko as in Goomsur, or Khonro as in Boad, and the chiefs of districts Patur instead of Bissoi.

The sacrifice in Chinna Kimedy is not offered to the earth alone, as in Goomsur and Boad, but to a number of deities, whose power is essential to life and happiness; of these Manicksoro, god of war, Boro Penoo, the great god, Zaro Penoo, the sun god, hold the chief place. The time of sacrifice is a time of excessive revelry, in which the women share. In some districts the victim, after certain ceremonies, is flung violently to the ground, and held or bound down while the flesh is cut off piece-meal. The

KHOND CHIEFS OF CHINNA KIMEDY IN THEIR ORDINARY COSTUME.

shreds thus procured are afterwards buried in their fields.

Several of the most inaccessible tribes have never acknowledged the authority of the Rajah, and generally the sacrificing Khonds of Chinna Kimedy do not visit the plains to attend the fairs, as do those of Goomsur and Boad, but dispose of their turmeric, their sole article of barter, for salt, cloth, or brass vessels, to traders from the plains, who are also very frequently professed kidnappers.

Considering the character given of the people, it was by no means improbable that resistance might be attempted, and, from our ignorance of them and of their country, the enterprise was an arduous one. It was therefore necessary to provide for all contingencies.

Nothing but the sternest necessity would have induced me in this good work to use force, but I felt satisfied that the resolute expression of the will of Government, with the assumption of a determined attitude, which would declare more plainly than words the fruitlessness of all attempts at opposition, was at once the most merciful and most effectual way of accomplishing our object.

I solicited the Governor-General's sanction to my proposed plan of operations, and it was conveyed to me as follows :

"Having every confidence in your experience and judgment, the Governor-General in council is pleased to authorise you to prosecute your measures in such a manner as may from time to time appear to you to be most expedient, keeping the Government constantly informed of your proceedings and progress. His Lordship is happy to remark that you are fully sensible of the desire of the Government that every method of persuasion shall be tried before having any recourse to force. Your camp and that of your assistant should be accompanied by at least a full company of regular infantry, and may be supported by the near neighbourhood of another, as suggested in your letter; and you should carefully avoid exposing yourself even to temporary discomfiture by employing a force on any occasion not sufficiently strong for every purpose. If you are resisted, and recourse to arms becomes unavoidable, the operations must be of so decisive a nature as to prevent the possibility of a protracted struggle."

Having made every advisable preparation, in November, 1849, I first entered the Chinna Kimedy hills.

The Khonds of Chinna Kimedy had been informed of my intended arrival, and they had plotted together how to turn me from my purpose. Finding all their stratagems in vain, and learning also that my camp was actually in march towards their hills, they resolved, as a last and desperate resource, on a general sacrifice of all their victims. This human holocaust might perhaps appease their deity, who would then, it was expected, interpose and hinder my coming; but at any rate, it would prevent the victims falling into my hands. Having learnt their intention, I pressed forward my march; and my somewhat sudden appearance with an armed force saved the lives of the intended victims.

I was fully alive to the necessity of proceeding with extreme caution on my first introduction to a wild and warlike race of men, who, of necessity, were prejudiced against me as a subverter of their ancient and cherished rite. I was sensible that any false or hasty step might plunge me into war with the whole of these tribes. Horrible indeed would have been a warfare in these dense forests and almost unknown mountains, where the climate was not the least deadly foe we should have had to contend against.

I had already conciliated and gained the confidence of Rajah Adikund Deo, of Chinna Kimedy, and of his tributary Rognat Deo, Tat Rajah of Guddapore, and their subordinate chiefs. This was a great step, for without their co-operation I could scarcely have hoped to accomplish the object in view, save by recourse to measures of severity painful even to contemplate.

I purposely avoided placing these rajahs at any time in antagonism with their hill subjects. I never allowed them to appear on the scene when the slightest coercion was needful, but confined all such acts exclusively to my own establishment; though following my invariahle course of procedure, I employed an intermediate cutchery agency as little as possible, and placed myself at once in direct communication with all classes.

From the very first, I openly, and in the most plain and intelligible manner, proclaimed the chief design of my appearance among them. Without any circumlocution, I told them that Government had sent me for the sole purpose of putting an end for ever to the inhuman and barbarous murders yearly perpetrated by them, and, if needful, to force the surrender of all the victims held in their possession, and destined to die this cruel death. All their other ancient usages, I impressed upon them, would be strictly respected; the Government being anxious to befriend them, and willing to assist them in every possible way. If any were suffering oppression, I promised that redress should be afforded, and justice meted out with an impartial hand, but insisted that Meriah sacrifices should be laid aside at once and for ever. This plain speaking was eminently beneficial. There was and could be no mistake in their minds regarding the intention of Government, and the presence of my armed escort added not a little to the weight of my declarations.

The Chinna Kimedy Maliahs are divided into seven districts, each ruled by an Ooryah chief, or Patur. These are subdivided into Mootas and villages, and these are governed respectively by a Khond chief, styled Maji, as in the Maliahs of Sooradah. Between these districts there is but little intercourse, owing to the feuds which are constantly occurring.

In the secondary range of mountains the villages are far apart, and the valleys, with very few exceptions, present a poor and barren appearance, contrasting, in this respect, most unfavourably with the more richly cultivated valleys of Boad and Goomsur. Water is less abundant than in the higher range, and thc country is uninviting in every particular, the eye beholding only a succession of mountains, thickly covered with the ordinary damur tree and with bamboo. The upper range, or table-land, is more picturesque; open valleys may there be seen in a high state of cultivation, and abundantly watered.

Throughout these mountains, human sacrifice, or female infanticide, prevails, with the exception of the large and fertile districts of Sarungudda, Chundragerry, and Deegee, where, happily, though surrounded by sacrificing and infanticidal tribes (the same race with themselves), neither is practised.

One of the most common ways of offering the sacrifice in Chinna Kimedy, is to the effigy of an elephant, rudely carved in wood, fixed on the top of a stout post, on which it is made to revolve. After the performance of the usual ceremonies, the intended victim is fastened to the proboscis of the elephant, and amidst the shouts and yells of the excited multitude of Khonds, is rapidly whirled round, when, at a given signal by the officiating Zani, or priest, the crowd rush in, seize the Meriah, and with their knives, cut the flesh off the shrieking wretch as long as life remains. He is then cut down, the skeleton burnt, and the horrid orgies are over.

In several villages I counted as many as fourteen effigies of elephants which had been used in former sacrifices. These I caused to be overthrown by the baggage elephants attached to my camp, in the presence of the assembled Khonds, to show them that these venerated objects had no power against the living animal, and to remove all vestiges of their bloody superstition.

In the large district of Mahasingi of Chinna Kimedy, one hundred purchased individuals were found, several of whom had marks of irons on their wrists and ankles, showing that they had been fettered to prevent escape. Only fifty-four of this number were destined for sacrifice, the rest had been bought as serfs, or for adoption (Possia Poes) either by the Ooryah inhabitants, a considerable and influential body, or by the Khond Majis. When I was fully satisfied that no foul play was intended towards these serfs, or Possia Poes, I ordered their re-delivery, first taking a registry of them, and receiving from their several proprietors the usual security, together with a written agreement, whereby they were bound carefully to preserve and produce them when required.

Daily, and almost hourly, were these wild mountaineers assembled in my camp. I wearied both the Khonds and myself with every argument I could think of to induce them to desist from a practice detestable in the sight of God and man. I recalled to their minds their own law of a life for a life, and challenged them to gainsay, if they could, its justice when applied to their own practice of slaying their fellow-creatures. I related at length how I had marched over Goomsur and Boad, and had swept away every Meriah from those countries, utterly abolishing the revolting rite; how their brethren in these neighbouring countries had most solemnly pledged themselves never again to sacrifice human beings, and how abundantly they had prospered in house and field since they had abstained from these horrid rites. I also very specially directed their attention to the fertile districts of Sarungudda and Deegee, where no human blood is shed to propitiate a sanguinary god, and where the fields are as productive as their own.

It would be tiresome to recount further details of our numerous interviews. I had not quite all the speaking to myself, for I invariably called on them to reply whether my speech was true or false, fair or unfair, and their general answer was, "It is true, it is just. Our fathers sacrificed and taught us to do so. The Great Government has sent a mighty chief to forbid the practice, and he must be obeyed. Let us then do as our brothers of Goomsur and Boad have done, and sacrifice buffaloes, goats, and pigs, instead of human beings."

After many and long conferences, an agreement was drawn up, as in Goomsur, and the document signed by all the principal men present, certain binding Khond formalities being observed to strengthen their pledge. It was then delivered to me by the chiefs, who turned round, and addressing the assembled Khonds, called on them to be true to the pledge which they had taken, not only for themselves, but for all. The chiefs were then invested with turbans. Presents of small sums of money and strips of red cloth were distributed, my tent and its contents inspected with wondering curiosity, and the assembly broke up.

As may very naturally be supposed, when it is considered that this was the first time they had been visited by any European, a considerable degree of reserve was frequently evinced by the people. Groups of men, women, and children sat gazing on at some distance, fearful to enter the camp. They had heard reports, spread by evil-disposed persons, that I was collecting Meriahs, for the purpose of sacrificing them on the plains to the water deity, because the water had disappeared from a large tank which I had constructed, and that my elephants required, periodically, a certain number of victims to be served to them as food.

No effort was spared to undeceive and conciliate all ranks, and to prove the honesty of our object in coming among them; and I am happy to think that the opinion entertained of us in the end was not unfavourable. The strictest discipline was maintained in camp, and in no part of the country did person or property receive the slightest damage.

Two hundred and six Meriah victims were rescued in this our first season in the hill tracts of Chinna Kimedy, though I doubt not that many were hidden from us, or carried to a distant part of the country.

From Chinna Kimedy I proceeded into the Boad hills, where my assistant, Captain Macviccar, had been travelling for some time.

The entire abolition of the rite of human sacrifice, which so recently prevailed throughout the Maliahs of Boad, ought to be a source of sincere congratulation to all Christians. Not one drop of blood had been shed this year at the shrine of a barbarous superstition, nor the least disposition evinced to break the pledge which the mountaineers had taken last year. The whole of these hills have been traversed, and the same pleasing results exhibited in every quarter.

It may be profitable to dwell for a little on the causes which have produced these most gratifying effects throughout the hills of Boad and Goomsur; for it appears to me of the greatest importance that the grounds upon which the suppression has been effected should not be misunderstood; and there seems great danger of misapprehension here, judging from an article that appeared in the "Calcutta Review," in which a magnificent display of language was united to a grievous perversion of facts.

In the Boad country, we ought in the first place to be most thankful to God whose bountiful harvest so powerfully and mercifully seconded our efforts; and to Him, too, we owe the suggestive fact that during the year the Khonds enjoyed immunity from all but the most ordinary sickness. Next we may ascribe much of our success to the felt and acknowledged power of the Government to enforce its will, which has always been unreservedly and without the slightest compromise declared to the Khonds, wherever met by myself or assistant, and proclaimed universally throughout the country.

There was no cautious inquisition recommended, as formerly, but the glaring fact was dealt with as an enormity which the Government neither could nor would suffer longer to exist. I mention this prominently, because the success which has attended my labours in Boad and Chinna Kimedy conclusively demonstrates the advantage of a firmer, bolder, and more decided line of policy than was deemed prudent in the days of our earlier connection with the tribes of these hills; and I venture to assert that if I had met with the same support in 1838-39 as I have since done, the good work of Meriah suppression would in all human probability have been as far advanced in 1841 as it was in 1849.

It could not rationally have been expected that moral persuasion alone—I do not, however, allude to that of the gospel—would or could with such rapidity convert a race of people shrouded in the grossest darkness from a superstition which for centuries had been riveting its chains upon their ignorant minds. I should indeed have been astonished if the prosperous results which have blessed our efforts on the hills could have been attributed exclusively to the weight and influence of the moral reasonings we adduced. Such discourses should never be omitted, and everywhere and on all occasions impressively urged; but had we rested on our arguments alone, I fear we should have effected little good. Hence, in assigning motives for abstaining from their ancient rite, the Khonds rarely made allusion to the moral persuasion that had been urged upon them, but laid marked stress upon the futility of all resistance, and the necessity of obeying the will of the Government.

I have not alluded to the great precursor of civilization—the Gospel—not because I am insensible of its fitness for these wild tribes (who have no predilection for Brahmins), but simply because it is not within the province of the Government of India to introduce any agency of the kind. I may, however, express the hope that in due season these poor savages will be visited by the teachers of a higher and purer wisdom than that of man.

In this season, from Chinna Kimedy and Boad, three hundred and seven Meriahs were rescued. About one hundred and twenty little children were placed under the care of the missionaries at Berhampore and Cuttack, at the expense of the Government. The married Meriahs, together with a number of youths of the same class, were settled

MERIAHS RESCUED FROM SACRIFICE.

in villages and set up as cultivators; others were apprenticed to different trades, and a few taught gardening; about fourteen were placed under the protection of private individuals, and twenty-five enlisted in my corps of Irregulars. The marriageable females are gradually being married to the Khonds of the infanticidal tribes, and others of suitable position, and are sought after as being the wards of Government, from whom they receive a fitting dowry. For the unmarried females and very young children, an asylum has been formed at Sooradah, under the superintendence of steady matrons, where the young women are practised in household affairs suited to their station; and from whence, at a proper age, the children are removed to the care of the missionaries for instruction.

The road which I recommended to be made into the Goomsur Khond Maliahs, by the Coormingia Pass, is in progress. One hundred and eighty-four miles of new routes, never before traversed by Europeans, were surveyed this season in the Khond country, and I recommended a road to be opened through the Goomsur and Boad Maliahs, to Sohunpore on the Mahanuddy, not only as facilitating, in a military point of view, the communication with Nagpore, but as opening up an easy line of road for the extensive traffic which is carried on by the Brinjaries, who are the chief purchasers of the salt manufactured on the sea-coast of the Ganjam district, and which they dispose of in the interior. The moral effect on the Khonds of a well-frequented road passing through their country would be very great.

Lieutenant Frye, an officer whose acquirements as a linguist were of the first order, laboured very zealously in the acquisition of the Khond language. He adopted the Ooryah alphabet as the best suited to express the sounds of this new dialect; and in order to facilitate the study of it by the Ooryahs attached to the agency, a vocabulary has been printed. The Meriah children at the mission schools at Berhampore readily understood and conversed with Lieutenant Frye.

The Khond Maliahs, always insalubrious, were most prejudicial this season to the health of the whole of the Agency Establishment. My assistant, Captain Macviccar, was prostrated with fever, the consequence of exposure and hard work in these unhealthy mountains, and in the month of May, 1849, he was sent to the Cape of Good Hope for the recovery of his health.

I struggled hard against disease, but at length was obliged to yield, and in the month of October following was ordered to the Cape on medical certificate.

I had again the honour of receiving the thanks of the Governor-General of India in Council, and the expression of the lively satisfaction which His Lordship experienced in learning the full and happy results of my exertions.

CHAPTER IX.

A VISIT TO THE TRIBES OF SOORADAH—PRACTICE OF INFANTICIDE—ORIGIN OF THE CUSTOM—REMEDY FOR FEMALE INFANTICIDE—APATHY OF THE MOTHERS—PREJUDICE IN FAVOUR OF MARRIAGE WITH WOMEN OF OTHER TRIBES—I PROPOSE A REMEDY—THE KHONDS AGREE TO REAR THEIR FEMALE OFFSPRING—MY REPORT TO GOVERNMENT—ESTABLISHMENT OF SCHOOLS—THE ASTROLOGER AT THE BIRTH OF AN INFANT—HIS PREDICTIONS—INFLUENCE OF THE NATIVE PRIESTS.

CHAPTER IX.

PREVIOUS to the events narrated in the foregoing chapter, I made a brief sojourn amongst the infanticidal tribes of Sooradah. These people never offer human sacrifices; their female infants are stifled at the hour of their birth, but they are not impelled to this barbarous usage by any religious motive. This practice is limited to a few districts in the hills of Sooradah and Jeypore. I frequently endeavoured to collect some authentic account of its rise and progress. It is not always an easy task, even in a civilised land, to glean from the more intelligent members of the community a correct narrative of the origin and progress of particular customs and observances which are rigidly and superstitiously adhered to; how great then must be the difficulty when we have to deal with a people whose moral and intellectual qualities are as yet undeveloped!

It must be borne in mind that these tribes are wild and barbarous in all their habits, retaining no traces of a lost civilization, and only the faintest recollection of ancestral traditions. They are not like the people of Rajahpootanah, who practise infanticide from well-understood and well-defined causes. I believe that in Sooradah poverty is the sustaining and originating cause of this great evil. It is the plea which they invariably set up, combined with the influence of long transmitted tradition.

"From time immemorial," they said, "we have done this thing—our fathers did so, we do as they did; we are poor, and we must follow their example."

Such was always and everywhere the language of the Khonds of Sooradah; and it is a remarkable fact, that it was never alleged by any one of them that they were moved to adopt this odious rite by motives of religion, or that their gods were in any way concerned in the matter. Several foolish legends were narrated to me. The following is that which seemed to find most favour amongst them.

In ancient times there was a man called Denko Mullico, who had four sons. Of these the three eldest begat eight sons each, and the youngest two daughters. The latter failed to obtain husbands, and in consequence became too intimate with some of their cousins. This induced the brothers, whose sons were not implicated, to deprive the brother, whose sons were, of all his property. Having learned how their paramours had been punished, their erring kinswomen drowned themselves in a tank called Reda Bondo. Afterwards the elders condoled with the disgraced younger brother; and, concluding that their alienation from, and contention with him, had been occasioned by his female issue, they decided that thenceforward their female issue should be destroyed, and solemnised this determination by invoking their deities Poboodi and Boropennoo. Since that time the practice of female infanticide has been maintained.

Such is one of many similar fables that are in circulation to account for the practice; but, as I have observed, it does not really spring from any religious feeling, but is generally the result of poverty. However, it is sometimes practised as a matter of convenience; for when a Khond of these Sooradah tribes marries, he is bound to give an equivalent to the wife's father for her. This can be reclaimed from the father, who is bound to repay it in the event of his daughter deserting her husband for another man. Such a contingency not unfrequently happens, and the paramour then becomes responsible to the father for the equivalent he has been made to restore.

Such settlements naturally give rise to endless difficulties and quarrels, which the people think to avoid by marrying women from distant places, for whom they give a much smaller sum than for those of their own tribes. They pretend, moreover, to regard it as degrading to bestow their daughters in marriage on men of their own tribe ; and consider it more manly to seek their wives in a distant country.

How to find an efficient remedy for this most inhuman crime has perplexed many sincere philanthropists. The Khonds asserted that they had tried, in obedience to orders, to discontinue the practice ; but that, nevertheless, their female children died, which they attributed to their having violated the solemn oath of their ancestors.

It might naturally be supposed that the women would have gladly aided us in our efforts to combat this evil, but their conduct, when appealed to, indicated utter want of sympathy ; the strong yearnings of maternal love seemed dead within them, and they spoke most heartlessly, apparently without the slightest feeling, of destroying their female offspring, or of suffering them to die in obedience to their husbands' commands. " How could they support them?" they demanded. Consequently the little creatures perished by scores. Mothers, too, were apathetic, and did not want girls—poor, and could not support them—cruel, and glad to get rid of them.

I endeavoured to remove from the minds of the men the prejudice against marrying females of their own community, and promised that I would procure for them wives from amongst our rescued Meriah victims. I hoped that such a relationship would bring us into closer contact, and enable the agents of Government to exercise a better supervision with reference to this prohibited custom. I knew that this system had been tried with a few, and had failed; but when greater numbers of Meriahs had become the wives of these Khonds, I felt confident that they would exercise a favourable influence, and become a check on the other inhabitants.

When I asked some of the men why they remained unmarried, they replied, because wives were so expensive. I showed them how the rearing of female children would render them much cheaper, but I do not think that my argument produced much effect —for we all know with what tenacity impressions imbibed in infancy cling to us through life.

I saw these rude people daily and hourly during my stay. I used every argument likely to carry weight, and illustrated my observations in such a manner as I hoped would implant them in their memories. I urged on all the duty of desisting from so horrible a practice, and assured them most solemnly that it was not their simple assent to my reasoning which would satisfy the powerful Government whose representative I was, but that the severest penalty would follow a violation of the promise they had intimated their readiness to make.

I very forcibly insisted on the certainty of immediate punishment succeeding the offence; as I knew, with savage tribes like these, fear at first must ever be our chief weapon. Their minds were pre-occupied, and though they professed conviction, I felt sure, in a little time after our backs were turned, that old thoughts and habits would gain the ascendancy; and that nothing but the dread of our vengeance would restrain their disposition for evil in this direction.

All the heads of families then signed an agreement binding themselves, under the severest penalties, henceforward to rear their female offspring. I promised to revisit their country soon, and anticipated the best results from their being now satisfied that in future ocular demonstration would alone convince me that they had fulfilled their pledge.

I tried hard to establish a registry of the men, their wives, and children, but was compelled to abandon the attempt. On discovering my intention, the people fled in great alarm, asserting that they were sure to die if I persisted in my design of numbering them.

Thoroughly to eradicate this evil, we must look to the diffusion of sound useful knowledge, especially amongst the rising generation. Fear has operated as a great restraint, and, as will hereafter be seen, has wonderfully abated the grievous evil. But permanent abolition cannot be expected from this source, neither would it be possible to deal with the offence in the regular course of law, for no evidence could ever be procured to insure conviction, and punishment, when inflicted, must necessarily be arbitrary.

I considered, and so reported to Government, at the close of my visit to Sooradah, that until we should be enabled to fix the language and establish village schools, and to introduce other wholesome measures for the moral elevation of this people, the best and surest means of abating the mischief consisted in maintaining a constant intercourse, and paying occasional visits, always insisting on seeing the female children, specially rewarding those who have preserved their infants; and punishing, in such a way as shall mark the extreme displeasure of the Government, the chiefs of those villages where the relative disproportion of the sexes should be so great as to leave no doubt of the destruction of the females.

I was fully aware how inadequate such measures appeared for the eradication of so prodigious an evil. I had bestowed all the attention due to the consideration of a subject so deeply interesting, and, after long and anxious thought, could devise no more hopeful remedies. Constant and vigilant supervision for the present seemed the only means of amelioration.

Two French Roman Catholic missionaries visited these people some years later, and established themselves at the base of their hills. By this time we were enabled to furnish them with the books prepared in the Khond language by Captain Frye, and with this aid they were soon enabled to commence teaching the children of those parents who would permit of their going to school.

They had abundance of scholars from the low country, and I understand that they were very successful in making converts; nor is this surprising, as they did not require renunciation of caste, nor did they prohibit many of the old Hindoo ceremonies. I must confess that the zeal and devotion of these missionaries were beyond praise. They lived in a kind of hovel, thatched with grass, a poor protection from the sun's burning rays; their food was chiefly rice, and of those comforts of civilized life to which in their native land they must have been accustomed, they were totally, I may say, voluntarily deprived; for though such were obtainable, they would not have them, preferring to give the natives the most complete example of self-denial. They were men of very superior education and manners, and their unwearied toil, their utter abnegation of self, and their gentle bearing towards all, must have extorted admiration from the warmest opponents of their creed.

The manner in which these infanticidal tribes of Sooradah pay homage to a superior is very remarkable, and to a stranger alarming. They rush into the camp in a compact phalanx of from sixty to two hundred men, uttering shrill cries, brandishing their battle-axes, and circling at a run, they advance and retire in imitation of a fight, and at last charge straight at the dignitary ready to receive them, to whom they present their offering of rice, a few addled eggs, and a kid. They then seat themselves on the ground, with the chiefs and Majis in front, and business commences.

When preferring a complaint, a Khond or Panoo will throw himself on his face, with hands joined, and a bunch of straw or grass in his mouth ; and I have more than once found myself in danger of a fall by the violent shying of my horse at the sudden appearance of three or four of these complainants throwing themselves on the ground before him.

I never heard of any tribe in Sooradah that put to death their male offspring, but I learnt from Captain McNeill that this occurs in some of the remote hills of Chinna Kimedy. The rite is practised in four districts, called respectively, Portya Desso, Soorah Desso, Thoomkah, and Korakah Puttah, in a manner almost identical. Whenever a child is born, a priest, or Dessawry, as he is called in that part of the country, is summoned, and consulted by the parents as to the future prospects of the new-born infant. The astrologer—for such is the pretended avocation of the priest—professes in a mysterious manner to consult the horoscope, and he also produces a kind of book (called Punjee), formed of dried Palmyrah leaves, on which are scrawled some sentences in the Hindoo character, intermingled with rudely drawn figures of mythical deities, demons, and devils, representing after their fashion good and evil spirits. Certain mumblings, and other ceremonies calculated to inspire the parents with a deep feeling of awe and reverence for the astrologer, are then gone through. An iron or bone style is finally inserted at random between the leaves of the book, and the fate of the unconscious baby is determined by the figure and words to which the style points. If the deity or sign thus capriciously selected represents good, the life of the little one is spared; if, on the contrary, it forbodes evil, the knell of death has sounded, and the child must die, else only evil will befall the family.

Such is the award of the astrologer, who includes the whole community in the malediction which is sure to follow if the child be permitted to live. All kinds of evil must ensue to the whole village; murrain will decimate their cattle, and drought reduce to sterility their lands. The point of the compass from which would flow these woes is also indicated. Who could brave all this wrath ?

The living infant is then placed in a new earthen vessel, the mouth of which is closed with a lid ; on it are placed some wild flowers and a small quantity of rice. The vessel is marked with alternate vertical streaks of black and red, then removed to that point of the compass which the astrologer has indicated, and there buried. After this a fowl is sacrificed over the spot which marks the infant's grave.

The only difference in these districts in their manner of practising infanticide is this, that in Korakah Puttah and Thoomkah, the priests, or astrologers, are Khonds, and do not use a book at all, but pretend, by some rude calculation, to know the position of some of the planets, and to ascertain their probable influence.

In these two last named districts, the child is wrapped in a cloth and buried, instead of being placed in an earthen vessel. The priests have, necessarily, great influence in their respective districts, and drive a thriving trade by practising on the ignorance and credulity of the tribes. Many years ago the Rajah of Jeypore, to whom these Khonds are in a certain measure tributary, sent an official, a Brahmin, to endeavour to suppress infanticide in one of these districts. The Brahmin met a melancholy fate—he was seized by the Khonds, bound hand and foot, and thrown over a precipice forty feet high. For this deliberate murder, the district was fined one thousand rupees (£100) by the Rajah, an amount equal to the whole wealth of the Khonds; but even such severe punishment had little effect in lessening the prevalence of the objectionable custom.

CHAPTER X.

ANTIQUITY OF HUMAN SACRIFICE—TRADITIONS—IDEA OF THE INFERIORITY OF WOMEN—SELF-IMMOLATION ENCOURAGED—MURDER AN ACT OF RELIGION—THE HILL TRIBES OF ORISSA—EXTRAORDINARY REPORT FORWARDED TO GOVERNMENT IN 1841—ITS CLASSIFICATION OF THE DEITIES OF THE KHONDS—NO TRACE OF THEM TO BE FOUND DURING MY SOJOURN AMONG THEM—DANCING AND DRINKING—SOME ACCOUNT OF SUNDERAH SINGH AND BAHA KHAN—NOTES AND QUERIES.

CHAPTER X.

THAT the "dark places of the earth are still full of the habitations of cruelty" will be the first thought in the mind of every reader of the painful narrative in the preceding chapters of the present work, which illustrate so strikingly the awful effect of ignorance and superstition on the human mind. The mysterious and still unsolved problem of the *felt* necessity of sacrifice to atone for sin, a feeling as old as time itself, will also recur to the mind, and many will ask again how it ever entered into the heart of man to conceive that God required a sacrifice at his hands, and that in no other way could his sins be washed out. It is undoubtedly a deep mystery; but the idea of sacrifice as a means of atonement being once present to his mind, it is quite intelligible that the costliest victim should be selected, and that man should be regarded as the most acceptable offering. Hence we find that the practice of human sacrifice existed not only among the most barbarous, but even among the most enlightened nations of antiquity. The oldest records of which we have any knowledge, the Hebrew scriptures, allude frequently to it, and it seemed most natural to the King of Moab, when consulting the prophet as to the best mode of pleasing the Lord, that he should offer to sacrifice his first-born in atonement for his own sins, "the fruit of his body for the sin of his soul."*

I need scarcely multiply instances; the Scythians, or Tartars, Scandinavians, Phœnicians, and Britons practised it frequently. Of classical examples I will only refer to the sacrifice to Artemis, by the Taurians, of the Greek sailors cast upon their inhospitable shores, and the hecatomb by the Emperor Augustus, to Julius Cæsar, of the three hundred citizens of Perugia. The waste of human life by the Roman emperors was as prodigal as is that of the King of Dahomey at a great festival. It had not the excuse and sanction of a religious observance in the majority of instances, and the amphitheatre received more victims than were ever offered to Baal and Moloch.

The extent to which this sanguinary practice took possession of the population of India, may be seen in their popular literature.

That admirable Oriental scholar, Professor H. H. Wilson, published an able article "On the Sacrifice of Human Beings as an Element of the Ancient

* Micah, chapter vi.

Religion of India,"* in which he refers to a legend in the first book of the *Rámáyana*, wherein a great chief is represented as selling his son for a hundred thousand cows to the King of Ayodhyá, as a sacrificial victim. A similar legend is to be found in the Bráhmana portion of the *Rig-veda*, from which I quote the following passage :—

" Harischander, the son of Vedhas, was a prince of the race of Ikshwaker. He had a hundred wives, but no son. On one occasion the two sages, Nárada and Parnada, were residing in his palace, and he said one day to Nárada,

" 'Tell me, why do all creatures, whether possessed of intelligence or devoid of it, desire male progeny. What benefit is derived from a son?'

" Nárada thus replied—

" 'A father who beholds the face of a living son discharges his debt [to his forefathers], and obtains immortality. Whatever benefits accrue to living beings upon earth, in fire, or in water, a father finds still more in his son. A father, by the birth of a son, traverses the great darkness [of both worlds]. He is born, as it were, of himself, and the son is a well freighted boat to bear him across [the ocean of misery]. What matter the impurity [of childhood], the skin [of the student], the beard [of the house-

* "Journal of the Royal Asiatic Society," vol. xiii., p. 96.

holder], the penance [of the hermit]? Wish, Brahmans, for a son, for he is a world without reproach. Food, vital air, vesture, dwelling, gold, beauty, cattle, wedlock, a friend, a wife, a daughter are all contemptible: a son is the light [that elevates his father] to the highest heaven. The husband is himself conceived by his wife, who becomes, as it were, his mother, and by her, in the tenth month, he is newly born; therefore is a wife termed genetrix *(jàyá)*, for of her is a man born again *(jáyak)*. Gods and Rishis implant in her great lustre, and the gods say to man, this is your parent. *There is no world for one without a son.*' "

This extravagant estimation of male offspring is a fixed principle in the Oriental mind, and prevails to this day in several nations, particularly among the Mahomedans of Turkey, the Hindoos of Hindostan, the natives of China, and the tribes of the Tartar Steppes. The corresponding depreciation of female offspring is well marked in these and kindred peoples, and, as a natural consequence, a woman is considered by them to hold an inferior place in creation. To such an extent is this conviction carried by the Mongols and other Tartar tribes, that the females, from the highest to the lowest, are not permitted to eat at a meal, till the males of all ranks have satisfied themselves with the choicest portion of the food.

It is stated in the *Actareya Bráhmâna*, from which I have already quoted, that the King, hearing this eulogium, at the suggestion of the sage who had repeated it, prayed to the Varuna for a son, promising to sacrifice him to that deity. A male child was in consequence born to him. But when reminded of his promise, he deferred the sacrifice from time to time by various ingenious excuses appreciable only by the Hindoo mind, till the boy, learning his destination, took to wandering from year to year, until he found a youth whom he bought of an impoverished father for a hundred cows, as a substitute. But the purchased victim contrived, by various devices, to delay his fate; and at last, by repeating verses in praise of peculiar deities, secured their interposition. A certain high official attending the sacrifice, who was blessed with a hundred sons, adopted the intended victim as his eldest. Fifty of the senior brethren did not approve of this promotion over their heads, which so excited their father's anger that he cursed them; and all the barbarous tribes, not excluding perhaps the Khonds, are said to be descended from the malcontents.

This tradition is preserved to demonstrate the honour in which the offering is held, the great value set upon him by the deities, and the evil results that follow any attempt to show him disrespect by its evasion.

In India, unquestionably, the sacrifice of human

beings took a strong hold upon the feelings of the people. The appearance of self-sacrifice was carefully kept up in the Suttee rite, which has counted its victims by thousands; and, at the feast of Juggernaut, at Pooree, near Cuttack, the devotees crushed beneath his chariot-wheels were always volunteers, or at least supposed to be so. Murder, it is well known, absolutely became a religion; and the principal article in the creed of the Thugs was assassination. The fact is, in the East life has been too lightly prized, and too readily thrown away. The Thugs were not more cruel than other Asiatics; but they were never known to exhibit any remorse for the many murders they had committed, so completely had their superstition got possession of their better feelings.

It must be a source of unfeigned satisfaction to know that this bloodthirstiness has ceased to disgrace the people of the East, as far at least as English influence prevails amongst them. The rite of Suttee has been abandoned for nearly thirty years. This great revolution was effected when Lord William Bentinck was Governor-General of India, and will ever be regarded as the brightest act of his reign. The colossal chariot-wheels of Juggernaut have not rolled over a human victim for a quarter of a century; and, thanks to the late Sir William Sleeman, and a devoted band of colleagues, the Thugs have been regularly hunted down. If the atrocious rite is ever performed, it is in out-of-the-way corners, and the victims must necessarily be very obscure. Sometimes, it is said, a stray member of the fraternity exercises his vocation on some of the rivers; and instead of strangling, he poisons his victim—but this is of rare occurrence, and in places not easily accessible to English officials.

It was not till long after Colonel Sleeman had commenced his most successful crusade against the Thugs, that it became known to the Government that other forms of this sanguinary superstition, as we have already described, were flourishing to a frightful extent in an almost inaccessible mountainous district stretching along the coast, part lying within the Bengal, and part within the Madras territory. Our little war with Goomsur, in 1836, may, therefore, so far be considered fortunate, inasmuch as it first made the Government acquainted with the fact that in the hill tribes of Orissa there were two forms of cruel superstition, exemplified, first, in the murder of female infants, and secondly, in the slaughter of human victims under circumstances of intolerable barbarity, thus rendering it imperative that immediate measures should be taken for the suppression of cruelties at which the human mind revolted.

It was by no means one of the least important results of the mission with which I had been entrusted, that I was enabled to acquire more exact and reliable information regarding these tribes and their inhuman sacrifices than had been previously communicated to the Government. The report of the Honourable Mr. Russell, who had so ably conducted the war, and by whom, as I have stated, Government was urged to appoint me to the charge of the hill districts, is in general accurate, offering such information as his opportunities—and no European before him had enjoyed greater—had afforded him the means of acquiring. The Khonds he classed amongst the most barbarous tribes of India; and the country they inhabited, besides being as wild as its population, was reported to possess a most pestilential reputation. The people were brave and savage, and possessed nothing that would induce a prudent government to provoke them. Nevertheless, there were many sound reasons, both of policy and humanity, to influence the ruling powers to attempt to bring these wild people under British supervision; not the least urgent of which was the abolition of those inhuman rites for which the Khonds had become infamous.

One report, forwarded to Government House in 1841, and published in a more complete form in 1852, in the thirteenth volume of the Journal of the Royal Asiatic Society of Great Britain and Ireland, must have startled the members of council, who knew the Khonds only as a tribe little removed from utter barbarism. The author of this report represented the Khonds as a refined people, overflowing with the most ingenious ideas. This was very much at variance with the notorious fact that they were without a written language, and that their religious ritual was as simple as it was savage. Nevertheless, this account was exceedingly comprehensive; and it was quite clear that its author had taken a great deal of trouble in its concoction.

One of its most remarkable features was the number of deities with which the Khonds were said to be provided—a feature, however, which puzzled only those who had no experience of native officials, and who did not know that Asiatic subordinates are possessed of resources, under difficulties, that throw the talents by which the Master of Ravenswood profited completely into the shade. Only let a sharp Hindoo or Mahomedan ascertain what kind of information you want, and that it will be for his interest to procure it, and you may rest satisfied the supply will fully equal the demand.

The mythology attributed to the Khonds of Orissa by the author of the report I have alluded to must be considered marvellous, when their present state of semi-barbarism and gross ignorance is borne in mind. They are furnished with a pantheon in which there are deities of various degrees of power, in a kind of railway classification. The first class consists of gods of rain, of new vegetation and first-fruits, of increase, of the chase, of war, called the Iron God (exactly as the Duke of Wellington was called the Iron Duke), and of boundaries; and they have a Judge of the Dead, to assist in their proceedings. The second class are composed of deified men, worthies of a primitive age, apparently too numerous to mention. The third class, sprung from the preceding two, are unlimited in number, but their chiefs are the gods of the village, of the hill, of streams, of the family or house, of the tank, of fountains, of the forest, of ravines, and of new fruits.

These poor and ignorant people, according to the account here furnished, are not only rich in deities, but as marvellously rich in souls, every Khond being gifted with four, and very remarkable souls they are. No. 1 is capable of beatification; No. 2 is attached to a tribe, and re-born in the tribe in a manner impossible to be explained; No. 3 endures sufferings and transmigrations, sometimes quits its corporeal tenement, to hold communion with a god, and sometimes to enter the body of a tiger; and No. 4 becomes extinct at its owner's dissolution.

In another point of view they are still more to be envied, for their beatified souls enjoy immediate communion with all the gods, live with them, "much after their fashion," and possess a certain amount of influence as intercessors for the restoration of lost relatives.

The form of worship must be something worthy of so extensive a pantheon, for every tribe invokes the souls of deceased ancestors, *in endless array,* at every ceremonial, after invoking the minor gods. As we have already been told that these worthies are unlimited in number, how the worshipper is to get through his ritual, if he does no more even than name his deities, it is impossible for me or any body else to say. In this religious observance, the author states that "the Khonds use neither temples nor images," a remark, however, which he subsequently qualifies.

In the course of my long inquiries and researches, I found nothing in the hill districts resembling the array of deities referred to in this report. I had with me several rescued Meriah victims, whose lives had been passed amongst the Khonds, whose ways were their ways, whose language was their language, yet not one of them had ever heard of this wonderful religious system, with its major and minor gods. Sacred images of the most barbarous type are to be found in most villages, and of these the priests, as ignorant as the rest of the people, can give no intelligible account. Indeed, save at the time of sacrifice, when wrath is to be averted, and their malignant deity propitiated by the offering of human blood, the Khonds are a most irreligious people. They rise early, smoke, go to their fields, and return in the evening, without performing any religious exercises whatever; and I am only surprised that in the list of deities furnished to the talented author of the essay I have noticed, a god of Drinking and of Dancing was not included.

Bacchus and Terpsichore have their votaries amongst these wild tribes at pretty frequent intervals, and then the distiller plies a profitable trade. Those who can keep themselves sober join in the national dance, to the national music of drum and lute. They dance alone, or in pairs (men only), and the step is a shuffling one, the eyes on the ground, the arms close to the body, and the elbow at an angle with the closed hand. The dancer (sometimes two) advances in a line to a certain point, which, having attained, he holds up his head, wheels round, and returns the way he came. In Boad and Goomsur the battle-axe is brandished during the step, but in other districts, Sooradah, &c., the dance is less warlike, the only accompaniment being the pipe, and sometimes the time is marked by the hand-clapping of the spectators.

The festivities of the Khonds usually terminate in universal drunkenness, for which I have never known them show the least signs of penitence or remorse. These orgies are evidently not regarded as displeasing to their gods, for no atonement is ever made for this oft-repeated offence. I took especial pains to become acquainted with their modern idols, but never could ascertain that they had anything more artistic than a log of wood, sometimes rudely fashioned after the manner of some animal's head, and only used on the occasion of the immolation of a human victim.

It is also asserted in the paper in the Journal of the Asiatic Society, to which I have been alluding, that a priesthood exists, which in its organization and labours corresponds with the elaborate system of idolatry provided for this semi-barbarous people. According to this narrative, the priest much resembles the medicine man of the North American Indian, seeking to discover, by certain mystic arts, the cause of the malady he may be called upon to cure, which he usually attributes to the displeasure of some god, or the magic of some enemy whrm the patient has offended.

According to this authority, there is a particular form of worship to every god, with particular traditions respecting him or her, all of which are given in detail, as well as ceremonials for different seasons. These are as carefully described as if the writer had lived the best part of his life in the Khond hills, and enjoyed the most perfect confidence of the leading members of the priesthood; yet it is well known that his personal experience of the Orissa mountains was very limited, especially prior to his first voluminous essay on the Khonds, ostensibly reporting the result of a survey made by him in 1837, in Goomsur and Boad, at the close of the military operations in those districts which had been almost exclusively directed by the Hon. Mr. Russell, under the orders of the Government of Madras.

In this paper, as in the later dissertation, there is the same elaboration of detail, though not to the same extent; and the author acknowledges that he has "unavoidably imparted to the subject a semblance of completeness, regularity, and system which does not strictly belong to it." Most assuredly it does not.

In the more complete essay of 1851, he apologises in these terms—"I fear that I have, perhaps unavoidably, imparted to the subject an appearance of theoretical completeness and consistency which does not strictly belong to it." Again nothing can be more true, and a stranger might find some difficulty in accounting for the facility with which a very limited personal knowledge, obtained under the double disadvantage of ignorance *both of the Khond and Ooryah language*, was turned to such extraordinary profit, should he be unaware of the imaginative powers of oriental subordinates, stimulated by a prospect of increasing their own influence, and turning that influence into rupees. The author has acknowledged his deep obligations to the late Sunderah Singh, and to Baba Khan, his principal native assistants, who contributed largely to the information thus published.

These two men were subsequently expelled the public service for gross corruption and extortion, and were the undoubted cause of all the troubles and anxieties which fell to the lot of the author of this elaborate essay in after times. They grievously abused the too great confidence reposed in them.

Sunderah Singh was an intelligent man, and might have rendered great service to the State; but he became the tool and accomplice of Baba Khan, a cunning, low-bred Mahomedan, who had been dressing boy and butler to the writer of the report, and was by him promoted to the more dignified office of Moonshee, in the establishment of the Government Agent. He knew not one word of the Khond language; but he knew the bent of his master's mind, and provided accordingly.

It is only thus that I can account for the comprehensive pantheon and worship put together in these essays, which cannot be identified as belonging to the

Khonds either by myself or by any one who has enjoyed similar opportunities of acquiring reliable information on the subject. My own experience was considerably greater than that of the writer, and my assistants were neither prejudiced nor careless observers ; more-over, I have reason to believe that I possessed the confidence of the chiefs and priests to an extent never before obtained by a European ; nevertheless I am not in a position to publish such a complete system of mythology as that to which I have been obliged to draw the reader's attention, or anything in the slightest degree resembling it.

No European has ever yet acquired a knowledge of the Khond dialect to be compared with that of the late Captain Frye, who was placed by me in charge of the agency, previous to my embarkation for the Cape of Good Hope. Now, this officer wrote a paper on the Ooryah and Khond population of Orissa, but with advantages far superior to those of the author of the essays adverted to. He is very far from imitating the "theoretical completeness and consistency" of the latter, when treating of the worship of the people. He says very little respecting it, simply because there is very little to be said. He gives four short lines in the Khond language as their creed, and describes their ceremonial in half a page. It is in every way different from the elaborate descriptions commented on, yet it was the result of a most careful personal inquiry conducted amongst a people whose language he perfectly comprehended; in addition to which, he was complete master of the Ooryah dialect, which is sometimes used in Khond assemblies.

In the Journal of the Asiatic Society of Bengal,* a paper was published, entitled "Notes and Queries suggested by a Visit to Orissa, in January, 1859; by the Rev. J. Long." It does not contain any reference to the system of mythology so carefully put together in the dissertations I have just noticed, although the subject must have been of special interest to the reverend gentleman who furnished this contribution. He asserts that Sterling's work is the only book written by a European that throws any light on the early history of the country, excepting Major Kittoe's account of his visits to the cave temples of Bhubanesar; those subsequently written only indicating that the writers knew little of the people below the surface.

Mr. Long mentions some of the peculiar customs of the country, but briefly; he evidently is not inclined to tell more than he knows, and does not care for being under obligation to the imagination of natives.

I have now done with this subject, which it was impossible for me to pass unnoticed. I must again

* New Series, vol. xxviii., p. 185.

repeat that I do not believe any European ever attained a greater amount of personal influence than myself, achieved, as has been shown in the preceding chapters, by very simple means; but with all the opportunities of acquiring accurate knowledge which I possessed, I was never able to obtain any information regarding the names and attributes of the various deities with whom the author of the papers referred to so liberally supplies the Pantheon of the Khonds.

CHAPTER XI.

CAPTAIN FRYE—HIS VISIT TO THE HILL TRIBES OF CHINNA KIMEDY—HIS ARRANGEMENTS ON BEHALF OF RESCUED MERIAHS—A SACRIFICE PREVENTED—VISIT TO UPPER GOOMSUR BY CAPTAIN MACVICCAR—ESTABLISHMENT OF SCHOOLS—STATE OF BOAD—KHONDS OF MAJI DESO—THEIR PRACTICE OF HUMAN SACRIFICE—PATNA—SUPPRESSION OF THE RITE THERE—CAPTAIN MACVICCAR'S VIEWS RESPECTING THE PRESENT CONDITION OF THE COUNTRY—RESULT OF HIS LABOURS.

CHAPTER XI.

I handed over the charge of the agency, during my absence at the Cape of Good Hope, to Capt. Frye, fully instructing him in the principles on which the work for the suppression of the Meriah was to be conducted. This admirable officer had always taken the deepest interest in our labours, and, being an oriental scholar of the highest rank, had occupied himself most zealously in the acquisition of the Khond language; and had already prepared an alphabet, using the Ooryah character, which was printed and used by the Meriah children in the missionary school at Berhampore.

On the 22nd of December, 1849, Captain Frye started on a tour through the hills of Chinna Kimedy. He stated, in his report to Government, that a large proportion of the victims he had rescued were women with young families, which they had borne to the men who had purchased them. He converted this state of concubinage—which, however, was in itself no security for the life of mother or offspring—into that of marriage, by a stipulation that the Meriah should be considered the wife of her owner, and the children his heirs. The paturs, or ruling chiefs, being duly held responsible for this compact, the families were settled in the country, and the Government of India relieved of the charge of their maintenance.

Adverting to this measure, Captain Frye considered that it provided security to the intended victims, and justice to their purchasers, and was of special advantage to the Government, in a financial as well as in a moral point of view, besides being of sound policy as regarded the abolition of human sacrifice. The primary motive of purchase is undoubtedly the immolation of a human being; and these women, as well as their offspring, were, previous to the intervention of the Government, liable to be offered up in sacrifice, their purchasers delivering them for that object to people in their village authorised to receive them, and absenting themselves during the consummation of the rite; while the relatives of both would avail themselves of the opportunity to share in the flesh of the victim.

Should the Anglo-Indian Government esteem it essential to the abolition of human sacrifice, it can claim the removal of every Meriah throughout the land; but were this right rigidly insisted on, very few if any of these families would be produced, and the great object indefinitely retarded by panic, by passive, or it might be active resistance.

Under these circumstances, it was highly desirable to ensure the security of life in the mode best suited to the comfort of these women, who cling to their masters and Khond associations; and I soon found on my return that when it was known there was no wish to sever these families from the father, but simply to secure their safety, the reluctance to produce them gave way, and large numbers were brought to me. This result afforded a striking proof that the fear of their families being torn from them is stronger than their wish to maintain the sacrifice.

The average price of the Meriahs was from fifty to eighty rupees, paid in most cases in farm stock and household stuff, and the cost not unfrequently reduces the purchaser to destitution. Unable to pay the customary dower required when a Khond contracts a marriage with his own people, he makes the purchased girl a temporary substitute till she is required for superstitious purposes.

Considering the moral darkness of these mountaineers, and their extreme poverty, it seems only just, in breaking down their prejudices, and forbidding an observance which they have hitherto regarded as essential to the removal of evil, to avoid, if possible, the infliction of pecuniary loss. Thus the Government is relieved from the burden of supporting women with young families, whose future settlement would be almost an impracticability; while the people, in relinquishing those set apart for sacrifice, and soliciting the privilege of considering them as their wives and children, appear to acknowledge the justice of the power which has so wisely and humanely dealt with them.

Independently of the pledges they have entered into for the abolition of the sacrifice, the restoration of their families has greatly facilitated this desirable object. The right of the Indian Government to carry the latter away has been established, and their permanent abode in the country rests wholly on the contingency of non-sacrifice. Their security from molestation is a condition of the comfort and welfare of the community. Safe themselves, they are regarded as pledges for the good faith of their people. By such an arrangement, the hands of the paturs are strengthened, since, should a disposition to sacrifice manifest itself, they will hold over the offenders, *in terrorem*, the summary removal of the wards of Government, and thus induce their possessors to acknowledge obedience to its will.

Such are some of the views of this excellent officer, who devoted himself energetically to strengthening and enlarging the work I had already so happily commenced. Captain Frye subsequently fell a victim to fever, contracted in the pestilential hills of Chinna Kimedy, and I can safely say that Government never lost a more zealous servant, nor a more accomplished scholar. He worked with all his heart in this good cause, and was one of the best and truest friends the Khonds ever had.

A curious circumstance occurred to this excellent officer when on the hills. He was informed one day of a sacrifice on the very eve of consummation; the victim was a young and handsome girl, fifteen or sixteen years old. Without a moment's hesitation, he hastened with a small body of armed men to the spot indicated, and on arrival found the Khonds already assembled with their sacrificing priest, and the intended victim prepared for the first act of the tragedy. He at once demanded her surrender; the Khonds, half mad with excitement, hesitated for a moment, but observing his little party preparing for action, they yielded the girl. Seeing the wild and irritated state of the Khonds, Captain Frye very prudently judged that this was no fitting occasion to argue with them, so with his prize he retraced his steps to his old encampment.

Scarcely, as he learnt afterwards, had he got out of sight of the infuriated mountaineers, when they said amongst themselves, "Why should we be debarred of our sacrifice?—see our aged priest, seventy summers have passed over his head—what further use is he? let us sacrifice him." So this old man was barbarously slaughtered, to satisfy their superstitious cravings.

These people were afterwards properly dealt with by Captain Frye, and sacrifice has never since been practised amongst them.

In 1850, I was still detained by ill health at the Cape, but Captain Macviccar had been enabled to return to Orissa, and to continue operations amongst the sacrificing tribes. He first visited Upper Goomsur, the scene of my earliest labours; and here he had friendly intercourse with the Khonds and their chiefs. The country enjoyed profound tranquillity, and the people were contented and prosperous.

The time had now come when we might fairly attempt to establish some village schools. Through the unwearied assiduity of Captain Frye, a sufficient quantity of school books in the Khond language had been prepared, and several of our rescued Meriah victims had been trained to officiate as schoolmasters and teachers.

So the opinion of the chiefs in council, assembled on the important question of educating their children, was asked. The opposition was most intense. Words can scarcely convey an adequate idea of the scorn and contempt manifested, especially by the elders of the tribes. This was to be expected; their eyes had grown dim in their old delusions, and they recounted ancient traditions foreboding direful calamities if once schools were permitted amongst them.

Time wore on, yet but little progress was made against this feeling. These men had passed their lives in darkness, and in darkness they wished to die. Any one acquainted with the phenomena of human progress from the barbarous to the civilized state, must be well aware how light and truth are at first opposed; and the pioneers of civilization and religion have generally been martyrs. There was no apprehension of such a contingency with us, but the difficulty was not the less great, and excessive patience was required to effect our purpose.

A favourable impression was made by producing a smart, well-dressed, intelligent Khond youth, one of themselves, who had been removed to prevent his being sacrificed, and had received a certain amount of education. In the presence of a great concourse of chiefs and people, he read a little tale to them in their own language. This evidently was a point in our favour, and some admitted that their sons would not be much injured if they could be made to do the same.

The elders sneered, and said it was all very well for lowlanders; asking, why should their sons be troubled with such learning? For centuries they had lived happily without it—and why should they not leave it alone? The hardening influences of self-satisfied ignorance had full possession of these old chiefs, and their gloomy superstitions and hatred of knowledge would end only with their lives. They were treated most indulgently; all were assured that as our only motive was their welfare, no violence would be done to their feelings, nor would force be employed to make them embrace our views. No effort was left untried to gain over individuals possessed of influence—for example in these cases is contagious; and if a beginning could be made, eventual success was certain.

At last one or two families actually promised to allow their children to attend; and it was considered an act of no ordinary courage when Gondo Naick, a man of some local importance, as chief of Oodiagherry, not only promised to send his own son, but to allow a school to be established in his village. This man had been more accustomed than most of the other chiefs to visit the low country, and his ideas were more liberal. But even he soon repented his offer; he visited Captain Macviccar the same night, begging to be released from his promise, lest it should compromise him in the eyes of his fellow-chiefs. He was, however, fully reassured, and a school was accordingly commenced; shortly after, a second was permitted, and soon we had four at work, with an aggregate of fifty-nine scholars.

Boad was the country next visited by Captain Macviccar, and the result of his tour through that and other lands is thus narrated in the records of the agency:

In 1850 no blood had been shed in Boad. The Khonds had renewed their pledges, and received tokens of the favour of Government, in reward for their good conduct.

In Maji Deso we broke fresh ground. This country is midway between Boad and Patna, and has also communication with Chinna Kimedy and Kalahundy.

These Khonds have never ceased to sacrifice, although in civilisation they have far outstripped their neighbours of the Boad and Goomsur hills. They possibly expected to escape our vigilance from the circumstance of their possessing but few Meriahs, the practice being only to purchase immediately preceding the sacrifice; and the offering is made to their deity, not as in Goomsur, for the purpose of obtaining cereal produce, but for general prosperity, and blessings for themselves and families.

From several of their chiefs I learnt their mode of performing the sacrifice; which equals, if it does not exceed in cruelty, the practice prevailing in other countries. On the appointed day, after the usual ceremonies, the Meriah is surrounded by the Khonds, who beat him or her violently on the head with the heavy metal bangles they purchase at the fairs, and wear on these occasions. If this inhuman violence does not immediately destroy the victim, an end is put to his sufferings by strangulation—a slit bamboo being used for that purpose. Strips of flesh are then cut off the back, and each recipient carries his portion to the stream which waters his fields, and there suspends it on a pole. The remains of the mangled carcase are then buried; funeral obsequies are performed seven days subsequently, and repeated one year afterwards.

Our exertions were attended with complete success. The few Meriahs that were in the district were delivered up, and the usual ceremony gone through of binding each chief by oath henceforward to renounce the Meriah poojah, with its connected ceremonies.

From Maji Deso the camp moved to Patna, and operations were commenced in the districts subordinate to the Tat or Vice-Rajah, named Laull Joogroy Singh.

The Khond villages and districts were successively traversed, and the same course pursued as in Boad and Goomsur. The suppression of the rite in these countries was well known, and the utter hopelessness of successful resistance to us fully understood; gradually the victims were brought in, and the chiefs were pledged to future abstinence. A list was carefully made of the several chiefs, villages, houses, &c., in this little tract, so that detection would be easy in the event of any recurrence to the proscribed rite—and this they well knew.

But without being too sanguine, it may be confidently assumed that, if proper care and supervision is exercised, the Khonds of this portion of the Patna Zemindary will never again venture to erect upon its pedestal their now dethroned idol. They are far superior to the Boad, Goomsur, or Chinna Kimedy Khonds; are better clad, have more comforts, use better implements, and pay taxes—a fact which speaks volumes for their advancement in civilization. We have never, as yet, encountered any hill tribes so well under subjection as these Patna Khonds.

It was necessary, for security, to remove thirty-three Meriahs; six were given for adoption; subsequently, at the earnest request, and on the security of the Tat Rajah, nine more were added to this list.

During our stay, many hundred people came to our hospital to be healed of their diseases. All that could be attempted for the suffering was most cheerfully done; medicine was dispensed to those requiring it, and attention was paid to the wants of all. In every way we endeavoured to convert our visit into a source of benefit, and the impression left upon the minds of men, women, and children was certainly not unfavourable to us.

Passing onwards to the next division of the same country, Patna, we removed fifty-six Meriahs, and re-delivered seven for adoption.

In these districts the Meriah sacrifice is performed under infinitely diversified forms. Stoning to death, beating to death with bamboos, and other barbarous modes of torture are resorted to. In two districts, called Gonkah and Toopah, it not unfrequently happens that sacrificing and non-sacrificing tribes inhabit the same village. This is a very remarkable circumstance, and occurs nowhere else in Khondistan. They live together in the most perfect harmony, interrupted only for seven days when a victim is slain; then the non-sacrificers remain within doors, and never pass through the front entrance of their houses, when they go to their fields, until the seven days have expired, when the funeral ceremonies of the victim are performed, and all re-unite as formerly. Meriahs are procurable at a cheaper rate in Patna than elsewhere; but why this is so, we were unable to discover.

On finishing our work in Patna, we crossed over into the Kalahundy territory, and pressed forward rapidly, owing to the advanced state of the season, to Moodunpore, the residence of a Vice-Rajah, named Koosung Singh, who was the nominal ruler of the three districts in which we desired to operate.

The names of these districts are Mohungerry, Oorladoney, and Tapparungah. The people expected us, and well knew what we wanted. We made a very good commencement, and received a large number of victims; but the lateness of the season, and a daily increasing amount of sickness, compelled us to be content with laying a good foundation for next season's labour.

In this year a great portion of Chinna Kimedy was revisited, and some new tracts brought under control. All that could be done eastward of Jeypore was accomplished, but unhappily human flesh was procurable from the frontier, though no blood, so far as we knew, was shed on Kimedy soil.

Sacrifice is in abeyance, if not abolished. The exchange and barter of Meriahs is almost neutralized, by the large number removed from the possibility of such a contingency; and a good understanding, undisturbed by any untoward events, is established amongst all classes. The country, in fact, is ours, and it only requires vigorous operations on the sacrificing frontier to render the rite, as regards Chinna Kimedy, one of the things of the past.

"I will here take the liberty," Captain Macviccar adds, "of stating my views regarding the sacrifice of human beings, because I believe there is a general impression that the cessation of the Meriah, or human sacrifice, implies a change in the religion of the Khonds. I venture to think otherwise, and to regard as chimerical the idea of moral improvement resulting from a prohibition of human sacrifice. For there is abundant evidence to show that this rite once prevailed in the low country, where almost every altar has, at one or another period, been stained with human blood. Foreign authority, it matters not whether Mahomedan or European, gradually drove it to the wild hills, where it now holds sway; and thus it was banished from the plains. But the same deity worshipped by the Khonds under many forms and names is just the bloodthirsty Doorgah of the Hindoos, the dread personification of malevolence.

"Now, when this deity is *obliged* to accept, as at the Doorgah festival of the plains, the blood of beasts, then human sacrifice is at an end. The appalling evil has ceased, but their religion has undergone no change. The Meriah, or human offering, under whatever name known, as it has various titles, is essentially the same in object, intention, and purpose as the animal sacrifice of the Doorgah festival.

"To this day the ritual of the Khonds is annually

celebrated in Pooramaree, the capital of Chinna Kimedy, in the low country, on the conclusion of the Dasserah festival, only a goat is now substituted for the more prized sacrifice. Just as in the Khond country itself, the non-sacrificing tribes, so called with exclusive reference to human beings, immolate the buffalo or bullock with the same ceremonial, while the sacrificing Khond offers simultaneously the human victim.

"The test of abolition is the substitution of an inferior animal as the victim; this has already taken place in Boad, Goomsur, and to some extent in Patna, but as yet in few places in Chinna Kimedy, just because the Khonds of this last named district can procure flesh from a neighbouring territory. The Khond will surrender his victims, and forbear the rite in his own person; nay, more, there may not be a single sacrifice throughout the length and breadth of a particular country, but if there be beyond its borders a spot where human blood flows, thither, if possible, its votaries will repair, and so long as they can procure, no matter from whence, a morsel of flesh to bury in the field, the rite remains intact, though the loss of human life may be to a considerable extent diminished.

"In every case, therefore, I hail the immolation of one bullock with more pleasure than the rescue of many victims, because it affords incontrovertible evidence that the primitive rite has yielded to the pressure from without. There has never been known a relapse where this has occurred. But this cannot be reasonably expected in Chinna Kimedy, nor can these vast regions be considered as fully and finally conquered, until an adequate force has been directed against, and an adequate impression made upon, the extensive and neighbouring principality of Jeypore. It is quite true that from season to season in Chinna Kimedy the sacrifice has greatly diminished, and to a very large extent the Meriahs have been placed beyond the reach of danger; but still I hold that the end and object of our mission is not fulfilled, so long as flesh can be imported from the Jeypore state. It constitutes a standing peril for the Khonds in Chinna Kimedy, and therefore the stronghold of Jeypore must be attacked without delay."

On returning to the lowlands, we passed through the infanticidal tracks, but owing to the alarming prevalence of small-pox, which had driven the inhabitants from their villages, it was not possible to do more than address to the few people we could meet some words of caution, admonition, and encouragement. There was a manifest increase of female children, which proved that the habit of destroying them had received a check, and more than this could not reasonably have been hoped for.

The result, then, of this season's labours were, under God's blessing, as follows:—In the hitherto unvisited districts of Maji Deso, Patna, and the remote hills of Kalahundy, a good foundation had been laid for the suppression of human sacrifices. We had renewed our intercourse, and consolidated our work with the Goomsur and Boad Khonds. A day of small things, not to be despised, had dawned upon Upper Goomsur in the establishment of schools. The slow olive had been planted, and races yet unborn might eat its fruit. A road was commenced from Koinjeur to Sohnpore, these two points being in the heart of the Khond country; the former in Madras, the latter in Bengal territory. Chinna Kimedy was searched, and many victims rescued.

I heartily wish all this could have been achieved at a less cost of suffering; but I found, on my return from the Cape, that fever and sickness had made such sad havoc as very much to lessen the sense of gratification with which I regarded these proceedings.

CHAPTER XII.

RETURN TO MY DUTIES AND PROCEED TO MAHASINGI—DESCRIPTION OF THIS DISTRICT—GO ON TO BISSUM CUTTACK—THE TAT RAJAH, NAIRRAINDUR DEO—HIS FEUD WITH THE RAJAH OF JEYPORE—RESCUE OF MERIAHS—RYABIJI—CHUNDERPORE—GODAIRY—LUMBARGAM—ATTACK ON MY CAMP—ATTACK REPELLED AND MERIAHS BROUGHT IN—BUNDARI—JUNNAH SACRIFICES—REVISIT SOORADAH—INFANTICIDE—FLIGHT OF KHONDS TO MY CAMP—ACCOUNT OF THE MERIAHS SETTLED IN THE LOW COUNTRY.

CHAPTER XII.

Early in October, 1851, I was again at my post, and on the 18th November ascended the Khond mountains, and passing through the heart of the Goomsur Maliahs, from whence the Meriah rite had been thoroughly extirpated, I entered the large district of Mahasingi belonging to Chinna Kimedy. The point of this extensive country which I first reached was Sarungudda, on the borders of Boad.

The tradition respecting Mahasingi is, that in former times it was the residence of a powerful Rajah who exercised sway over the districts of Mahasingi, Barcooma, and Sarungudda. He died, leaving three sons, the eldest to rule over Mahasingi, the second over Barcooma, and the third and youngest over Sarungudda and Kurtolly. The latter, being a good and just man, and much esteemed by the Khonds, endeavoured to wean them from the sacrifice of human beings, but not succeeding, he prepared, with all his family and followers, to leave them, and had made one march towards the plains, when they, moved with sorrow at the sight of their departing chief, and having no love for his brothers, into whose hands they were sure to fall, entreated him to return, which, after much persuasion, he consented to do, on condition of their forsaking human sacrifice. To this they agreed, and bound themselves by the most solemn oaths, which, to this day, they have not broken; and the descendants of the younger brother, Cheytun Patur and Dawdy Patur, now rule over these non-sacrificing tribes, who are as courageous and as prosperous as their neighbours.

I found that Mahasingi had suffered grievously from long-existing feuds, in consequence of which much land had become waste and neglected. On some of these lands I was able to settle eighteen of our Meriah families—in all, fifty-three persons; and near this settlement, in an island formed by a mountain stream, on the site of the ancient fort of Mahasingi, I built a bungalow. According to popular tradition, the place had been taken possession of by demons, the island deserted, and the fortress allowed to go to decay.

From Mahasingi, I penetrated through an unexplored country to Bissum Cuttack of Jeypore, where I found the Tat Rajah, Nairraindur Deo, in considerable uneasiness respecting the object of my mission, for the proclamation regarding it which I had issued some months previously had not reached him. He was at feud with his superior, the Rajah of Jeypore, who had, about eighteen years before, on pretence of arrears of tribute, seized and imprisoned Nairraindur Deo's father, who, after six years' incarceration, had died in confinement. During that time, and the six years following, the Rajah of Jeypore administered the affairs of Bissum Cuttack, keeping Nairraindur Deo, who was then young, under restraint; but after the death of the Tat Rajah, the population of Bissum Cuttack had expelled the Rajah of Jeypore's people, and brought Nairraindur Deo to his fort, where they had since maintained him.

Thinking I had come to take part against him, he had some hesitation in visiting me; but I soon satisfied him as to my intentions. Confidence having been established, he zealously set about assembling the Khond chiefs of his country, himself in person going to those distant villages where any reluctance was shown by the inhabitants to come to me; for he holds the hill tribes in complete subjection, and has a following of about five hundred matchlock men.

In his house I discovered a youth who had been purchased by him for sacrifice, and had undergone all the ceremonies preparatory to his immolation to the god of battles, Manicksoro, in anticipation of a collision with the troops of the Rajah of Jeypore. This very nearly occurred, for taking advantage of my presence, the Rajah dispatched a force to Bissum Cuttack; but I would permit no hostilities, and the detachment he had sent was not strong enough to effect its purpose without my countenance. Nairraindur Deo was quite willing to pay the customary tribute to his superior, but he demanded a settlement of accounts for the twelve years the Rajah had administered the revenue of Bissum Cuttack.

I saw a very large proportion of the inhabitants of this hill Zumendari, and of the adjoining Moota of Doorgi, and I learnt with much satisfaction, from concurrent testimony, that with the exception of two small Mootas, Ambadola and Kunkabody, bordering on Chinna Kimedy, the Meriah sacrifice had ceased for more than two generations, though some of the villages still participated in the cruel rite by procuring the flesh of Meriahs from the neighbouring district of Ryabiji. This flesh, to be efficacious in securing the fertility of their fields, must be deposited in the ground before sunset on the day of the sacrifice, and to ensure this, instances are related of pieces having been conveyed, by relays of men, an incredible distance in a few hours.

From the two small districts above named, four

Meriahs were removed; all, I believe, that were in the possession of the villagers.

From Rajah Nairraindur Deo I received the youth destined by him for sacrifice. The victim, when offered by the Ooryah chief, is called Junnah; and this sacrifice is performed on important occasions, such as going to battle, building a fort in an important village, and to avert any threatened danger.

I lost no opportunity of impressing upon the inhabitants, collectively and individually, the heinousness of the crime of human sacrifice, and made them aware that those who were present at the immolation of the victim, and appropriated part of the flesh for their fields, were little less criminal than the actual sacrificers. At the ceremonial of leave-taking, I presented the Rajah with a detonating rifle, which pleased him much.

The inhabitants of this district are, in civilization, far in advance of the Khonds of Boad and Chinna Kimedy. Their language is that of the Ooryahs, whom they strongly resemble; and they have abandoned the Khond dress. This arises from the large traffic they carry on with the low country, and their constant intercommunication with the Ooryahs. Their land especially appears well cultivated, when compared with the dense jungly tracts which separate Chinna Kimedy from Jeypore.

On the 17th of December we left Bissum Cuttack for Ryabiji, travelling in an easterly direction, through a mass of jungle and rugged hills wooded to the top. The country is badly watered, and the only cultivation is found round the villages, which are far apart.

In the Moota of Ryabiji, the Meriah prevails to a great extent, and the natives resemble in appearance and character those of Chinna Kimedy, but the dialect they speak is different, and could with difficulty be understood by my Khond interpreters. Here, ignorant of localities, I was obliged to feel my way cautiously, for at the commencement of my operations the Ooryah chiefs, not fully comprehending what was expected of them, were of very little use. Gradually their confidence increased, and eventually sixty-nine Meriahs were rescued from Ryabiji Moota.

Here, as in all other places, the same language was held to the Khonds respecting the obnoxious rite. All who had brought in Meriahs, and the chiefs and principal men of the several villages, signed the usual pledge to abstain for ever from the abominable sacrifice.

A romantic incident occurred to one of the victims rescued from the borders of Ryabiji, which proves how short a time is required to effect a complete revulsion in a mother's feelings towards her child.

Whilst under the spell and thraldom of the Meriah delusion, a woman views not only with composure, but with pride and satisfaction, the sacrifice of her offspring, regarding such an offering as held in especial favour by the gods, and the victim as more than human.

The subject of the following adventure had clearly such feelings, when first I took her and her three young children from a village in Ryabiji. They were a Meriah family, and remained with my camp until I returned to the plains. It was only there for the first time that she made known to me the fact of her having another son, a boy of about six years old, whose existence, as well as his person, had been concealed from me. The body had been presented to their deity—the earth goddess—and by her had been approved and accepted as a fit offering.

She now earnestly implored me to send a party to endeavour to rescue him. I was most reluctantly compelled to refuse, as the very advanced state of the season would have proved fatal to any detachment I might despatch on such an errand; moreover, I desired to avoid risking any hostile encounter with the Khonds, who were still labouring under the excitement of our first visit amongst them for the avowed object of suppressing their much-loved rite. I promised, however, a very early expedition next season, when I hoped we should still be in time to save her child's life. This promise failed to satisfy the mother, who then resided at our asylum in Sooradah.

Immediately afterwards, although the rains were at their height, for it was the monsoon period, it was reported to me that she had escaped from the asylum, but without taking her children. I could do nothing but hope for the best, and heartily desire the success of her efforts, for it was not hard to guess what was the object of her flight.

A month passed away, but there was no news of the fugitive, and I began to despair of ever seeing the woman again; but about the fortieth day after her flight from Sooradah, she appeared before me, bringing her little boy with her, much to my gratification.

I learnt from her own lips the history of her perilous adventure. She said that she could neither rest nor sleep (it was evident that a great and complete change had taken place in her feelings since she had been with us) while she knew her son to be in danger of being sacrificed. Her distress at last became so overpowering that she resolved to save him at all hazards to herself.

She fled from Sooradah, and in due time reached the hills, though not without difficulty and danger, tigers and snakes abounding in the jungle. She dared not let herself be seen by friendly tribes, lest she should be seized and sent back as a runaway Meriah; and if the wilder or unpledged tribes had caught sight of her, she would at once have been delivered over to her former owners; so the danger was equally great from friend or foe.

The poor creature, therefore, travelled only under cover of the night; and what nights they were at such a season! A perfect deluge of water was pouring from the heavens; the mountain torrents were roaring, and bursting from their banks; and the wild beasts howling in concert with the elements. But this brave woman, the instincts of whose better nature had now for the first time been awakened, was not disheartened. She crouched in the forests by day, lest she should be seen, and pursued her journey only when the people of the villages were asleep—subsisting on what wild roots she could find, when the small stock of parched rice which she had carried away from the asylum was exhausted.

At last she reached her village, and hovered about it for three days, not daring to enter when the inhabitants were there, but waiting her opportunity when, as is generally the case in the rainy season, all the villagers should be absent in their fields. The fortunate moment arrived; she saw her son, and no one being present, she seized him, carried him off, and fled with all the strength which desperate resolution lends to courage.

In a few nights she reached the territory of the friendly tribes, and had nothing more to fear. She could tell them what she had done, and pray them to help her back by easy stages to the first military station. This of course they readily did, and I do not know that I ever felt more satisfaction than when I welcomed this heroic woman and the little son she had so nobly rescued. I found her worn to a skeleton by suffering and exposure, sufficient to have made the strongest man succumb. It should be remembered that not four months previously she would have gloried in her son's sacrifice.

It will not displease the reader to know that she and all her children were well cared for, and, with the usual liberality of the Indian Government, comfortably provided for for the remainder of their lives.

From Ryabiji to the Moota of Chunderpore, our course was to the north and east; the country being of the same inhospitable character, afforded no supplies of any kind. There my escort of sepoys became so disheartened and prostrated by sickness, both officers and men, that I was obliged to send them to the plains, retaining only a few of the most hardy of the men; but they too, and my establishment generally, soon gave way, and provisions becoming scarce, I found it necessary to push for the more open country of Godairy.

At Godairy, a large Ooryah village on the banks of the Bangsadara river, the country is well cultivated, and has a mixed population of Khonds and Sourahs. A considerable traffic in rice and other grains, and timber for building purposes, is carried on with the plains. The Khonds, comparatively a civilized race, after some little evasion and procrastination, delivered up their Meriahs to the number of thirteen, and readily entered into the usual agreement to abandon the rite of human sacrifice for ever.

Here I commenced the erection of a bungalow of three rooms. It was built on posts of about eighteen feet high, with walls of planks, and a thatched roof, after the fashion of the Khond houses, to which was added an open verandah all round, six feet high. It was intended as a rest house, and as a mark to the Khonds that our visits were not temporary merely, but that we might be found among them at any time.

At this place I first came in contact with the Sourah race. They are of a fairer complexion, and their features, resembling the Gentoos of the plains, have a better expression than those of the Khonds. They speak a different dialect, are less dissipated in their habits, and consequently more athletic in their persons, which they adorn with beads and bangles; this custom, however, is more common with the women than with the men. Their arms are the battle-axe, bow and arrow, though a few have matchlocks. They are professed thieves and plunderers, and are the terror of the inhabitants of the plains. Even the Khonds, so ready to fight among themselves, would rather avoid than seek a quarrel with the Sourahs; the latter generally make their attacks under the cover of darkness, a mode of warfare rarely adopted by the others.

The Sourahs do not sacrifice human beings, nor is female infanticide known among them, but some of them participate in the Meriah, by procuring flesh from places where the sacrifice occurs, and burying it in their fields. They did not seem to attach much importance to the rite, and at once promised to have nothing more to do with it—refraining from it even as spectators.

From Godairy, where I left some sick men, I proceeded on the 14th of January in a north-easterly direction, over an unexplored country, and by difficult paths, to Lumbargam, of Mal Moota, of Godairy; one of a cluster of six villages, each occupying a distinct basin or dell, surrounded by rugged wooded mountains, that communicate with each other by paths difficult for any but a mountaineer to travel.

These villages are generally at feud with each other, but on the occasion of my visit they were closely united to repel the retribution which they supposed I had come to exact for the murders, in which all were more or less concerned, of three messengers of the Nigoban manager of Godairy, who, under cover of being the bearers of a proclamation respecting the Meriah, had extorted buffaloes, goats, and brass vessels from the Khonds.

It is not easy to convey a just notion of the patience, perseverance, and forbearance required in dealing with these wild people. They are suspicious to a degree, easily moved to violence, and act apparently more from animal instinct than from the reasoning of human beings. For eleven days I was encamped in rice fields, which, during that time, were twice flooded with rain. I had also to cut a way, not without considerable difficulty, through the jungle, over two ghats, leading to three of the principal villages, in order to communicate with and undeceive the people. Either they did not comprehend me, or there was some underhand influence at work which I could not detect. These Khonds were the wildest I had yet met with; their country has no superfluity of produce for sale or barter, and they seldom leave their own bounds except to fight with a neighbouring tribe, which they are prone to do on very slight provocation.

After repeated threats and demonstrations, emboldened by the smallness of the force at my disposal, about three hundred of them assaulted my camp, shouting and yelling more like demons than men. The attacking party were supported by as many more, uttering cries of encouragement from the rocks and jungle that surrounded the camp; but a steady and resolute advance soon drove them off. A few shots completed the rout, and we pursued them rapidly over the mountains till they were lost in the jungle dells on the other side.

The next day delegates arrived from the several villages of the confederation, and the day following all came in, made their submission, delivered up thirty-three Meriahs, and entered into the usual agreement to entirely abandon the sacrifice. Confidence was established, and my camp crowded with our late foes, gazing with astonishment at all they saw. The Chief of Lumbargam, Brino Maji, who had been the first to submit, had the Sari, or turban, conferred on him as a token of recognition of his authority on the part of Government, and acknowledgment of fealty on his.

The whole neighbouring population were intensely watching the result of the struggle at Lumbargam, the successful termination of which exercised a most favourable influence on the proceedings that followed in the large Moota of Sirdapore, where the Khonds had declared that they might as well fight against the sun as offer resistance to me!

From Lumbargam I proceeded in a southerly direction, in three marches, by the most difficult paths I ever travelled, to Sirdapore, where all the Khonds were ready to wait upon me, with the exception of those of Dagodi, who, not till the third day after my arrival, came in with their Meriahs. From them I learnt that they had bribed one of the inferior Ooryah officers of the district, who had considerable influence with them, to keep me from their village, and so enable them to retain their victims. I caused the amount of the bribe to be repaid in my presence, and sent the offender to his master, the Rajah of Jeypore.

I found Sirdapore distracted by internal dissensions; many lives had been lost, villages burned, and a considerable portion of the land left uncultivated for several seasons, to the great distress of the people. These feuds I had the happiness of healing. I also settled many desperate quarrels of old standing in other parts of the Khond country, and thus restored to their villages and fields several hundred families who had been driven by their more powerful opponents to take shelter in the jungles, where they were exposed to great hardships, for they lived in temporary huts, raised in unassailable positions, and subsisted on such jungle fruit and roots as they could find.

Where the disputants are more equally matched, the feud is kept alive by their plundering each other of cattle, and by acts of hostility; for although all parties may be most desirous of a settlement, it is not easy to bring them together. Indeed, it has occurred repeatedly that the very men who have come secretly to me, begging that I would compose their quarrel, have been the loudest to disclaim in public all desire for an arrangement, preferring, as they said, to fight it out.

When, however, the parties finally agreed to submit their feuds to my arbitration, I assembled the chiefs of as many neutral tribes, and Ooryah Paturs, as were within reach, and forming a sort of court under some convenient tree, heard from each side the origin and details of the quarrel, the number of cattle taken, and the amount of lives lost by each. The latter I generally found very evenly balanced, for they are very unwilling to admit having lost more men than their adversary, and account only for those openly slain. People who have been waylaid and secretly murdered are passed over as having been devoured by a tiger or snake. There is of course much loud and angry disputation, but eventually the record of their respective losses in cattle or articles, reckoned by knots on a cord made from the bark of a tree, having been handed to me, I called upon the Khond and Ooryah chiefs to give their opinion as to what the award should be; and this being duly settled and pronounced, the opponents are brought together, swear eternal friendship, hug and embrace each other, and having received from me a small money present, they return to their homes rejoicing that they can now go to their occupations without fear of being waylaid.

The people of Sirdapore, with the exception of two or three villages bordering on Chinna Kimedy, are on a par in point of civilization with the Khonds of Bissum Cuttack and the lower parts of Godairy. They do not rear Meriahs as in many other places, but procure sacrificial flesh from Ryabiji and Chunderpore.

When a sacrifice is considered necessary, they unite and purchase a victim for the occasion; but at once, without any hesitation, they agreed to abandon the rite, and all participation in it, for ever. They came freely into my camp, and I have no reason to doubt the sincerity of their promise.

On the 6th of February I returned to Godairy to procure provisions and to forward the work of the bungalow. From thence I marched in four days by Seirgooda, Bijipore, Kiloondi to Chunderpore, one of the strongholds of the sanguinary superstition, in this second in importance only to Ryabiji. The Khonds came to me much more readily than on my first visit a few weeks before, and delivered up their Meriahs. Several of the chiefs on being asked to sign the pledge, which was always carefully explained to them, to abandon the sacrifice, answered,

"Many countries have forsaken the Meriah sacrifice at the orders of the Great Government, why should not we do so also?"

The people of Bundari, one of the principal Khond villages of this Moota, refused to come to me, or send me their Meriahs. They fled, with everything they could remove, to their concealed fastnesses in the mountains, which I failed to discover. In riding in the direction of Bundari, I discovered the cause of their flight, in a post spotted with blood, to which a victim had been fastened by the hair, the head being there still suspended, and the sacrificial knife attached to it. This piteous spectacle agitated the whole camp, and all felt they could not leave Bundari till the five victims still in the possession of these barbarians were rescued.

The sacrifice which had taken place, called Junnah, is performed as follows, and is always succeeded by the sacrifice of three other human victims, two to the sun to the east and west, and one in the centre, with the usual barbarities. A stout wooden post is firmly fixed in the ground, at the foot of it a narrow grave is dug, and to the top of the post the victim is firmly fastened by the long hair of his head. Four assistants hold his outstretched arms and legs, the body being suspended horizontally over the grave, with the face towards the earth. The officiating zani, or priest, standing on the right side, repeats the following invocation, at intervals hacking with his sacrificing knife the back part of the shrieking victim's neck:

"O mighty Manicksoro, this is your festal day." (To the Khonds the offering is Meriah, to the Rajahs Junnah.) "On account of this sacrifice you have given to Rajahs countries, guns, and swords. The sacrifice we now offer you must eat, and we pray that our battle-axes may be turned into swords, our bows and arrows into gunpowder and balls, and if we have any quarrels with other tribes, give us the victory, and preserve us from the tyranny of Rajahs and their officers."

Then addressing the victim, he added, "That we may enjoy prosperity, we offer you a sacrifice to our God Manicksoro, who will immediately eat you, so be not grieved at our slaying you. Your parents were aware when we purchased you from them for sixty gunties (articles), that we did so with intent to sacrifice you; there is, therefore, no sin on our heads, but on those of your parents. After you are dead, we shall perform your obsequies."

The victim is then decapitated, the body thrown into the grave, and the head left suspended from the post till devoured by wild beasts. The knife remains fastened to the post till the three sacrifices already mentioned have been performed, when it is removed with much ceremony. The knife and post employed in the sacrifice I have alluded to are now my property, and have been lent by me to the Indian Collection in the Crystal Palace, where they may be seen.

I used every exertion to communicate with the people. I even offered them pardon for the grievous offence they had committed; but it was of no avail. Provisions became scarce, sickness prevailed to an alarming extent, and as the only means of saving the lives of the three victims whose sacrifice would have assuredly followed that which had been already perpetrated, I, though most reluctantly, ordered the village of Bundari to be burnt, and also eight posts, the relics of former sacrifices, to be destroyed. The successful evasion of this people would, if left unpunished, have set a most injurious example to the whole sacrificing population.

Leaving Bundari on the 24th of February, I passed

RESCUED MERIAH VICTIMS.

through the secondary range of hills of Chinna Kimedy, inhabited by sacrificing tribes, and was gratified to find that they continued true to their pledge of forsaking the obnoxious rite.

The lateness of the season, and the difficulty of procuring a sufficiency of water for my camp in the infanticidal Maliahs, prevented my visiting those tribes; but on my arrival in Sooradah, below the ghats, many of the chiefs and a great number of the Meriah females who had been married to Khonds of these tracts, visited me with their children, to receive the usual presents of clothes, &c. From them I learned with satisfaction that female children were now generally preserved, and when any were destroyed, it was done with great secrecy, not openly, as in former times. The officer I had employed in superintending them confirmed this report.

The number of real Meriahs rescued this season was one hundred and fifty-eight; the number of Possiahs registered and restored to their owners, sixteen.

It is deserving of remark that four Khonds, who had formed attachments to Meriah women, fled with them to my camp in Jeypore for protection, preferring to forsake their country and people rather than that their wives (as they may be called) and children should run the risk of being sacrificed. Two Khond women also fled from Bundari with Meriah youths, from motives of humanity, as they stated to me, but I think they were influenced by a more tender feeling. Several similar instances occurred in my various journeys, but not to the extent which might have been expected, owing to a belief generally entertained by the intended victims that, having once partaken of Meriah food, rice, turmeric, &c., that had been prepared with certain ceremonies, they could have no longer any inclination to escape. This impression is indicated in the following incident:—

In 1839, three young women of the Panoo caste of the plains were hired, by a seller of salt fish and salt, to carry his merchandise into the Khond Maliahs, where, having sold his goods, the villain sold the women also. On the complaint of their relations, they were sought after, recovered, and sent to me by Sam Bissoi, chief of Hodzaghur. On my questioning them, they said they had twice attempted to escape, but were brought back, when the Khonds compelled them to eat of the Meriah food, after which they became reconciled to their fate, and lost all inclination to escape.

The districts of Ryabiji and Chunderpore have been the strongholds of the sacrifice in Jeypore. Out of the one hundred and fifty-eight Meriahs rescued during the season, one hundred and four were from these two districts. They have now been traversed throughout. We know all the principal villages, and their chiefs, and they know something of us, and of our object in coming to them. The first operations among a wild and strange people, always the most difficult and most hazardous, having been successful, those of succeeding seasons, if the same principles are adhered to, are mere gleanings; but the perils of the climate must always remain the same.

The Meriah females were more eagerly sought after in marriage by the Khonds of Sooradah and Chinna Kimedy than formerly, and several have been married to Meriah youths settled as Ryuts in Goomsur and elsewhere.

Such families, formerly settled as Ryuts in Goomsur, are doing well. About a third of the number—those originally established—have this year, for the first time, paid the rent of their land. From some the full amount was collected, but remitted, to support them till next harvest, and for seed. Others, more recently settled, are maintained at the expense of the State. By the next harvest, I anticipate that nearly all will be in a condition to support themselves; but they are generally idle, restraint of any kind is distasteful to them, and they miss their favourite toddy, and the many esculent roots which abound in the mountain forests.

Sickness was, as usual, this season, our deadliest

foe. My escort of native troops was soon disabled, and *hors de combat.* I had no alternative but to send them to the plains. I need not say how much my movements were crippled, nor could I have accomplished what I did but for the invaluable aid of my own faithful Irregulars, who were so well acclimated as to be fit for any duty.

Of the four European officers with the regular troops, one died of fever, and the other three were sent off to various climates to renew their shattered constitutions.

I remained with my establishment during the rainy season in the low country, preparing for the next season's labours.

CHAPTER XIII.

I REVISIT THE INFANTICIDAL DISTRICTS—RESULTS—AGAIN ENTER CHINNA KIMEDY AND PREVENT A SACRIFICE IN BONDIGAM—FURTHER SUBMISSIONS IN THESE DISTRICTS—RESTORATION OF SOME ORIGINAL MERIAHS—CONDUCT OF THE TRIBES OF TOOPUNGA—COLLISION AND SUBSEQUENT SURRENDER OF THESE TRIBES—PROCEED TO BUNDARI IN JEYPORE—REVISIT RYABIJI—THE ONE EXCEPTION IN JEYPORE—SOME ACCOUNT OF THE KOOTIAH KHONDS—KALAHUNDY—PATNA—RUINED TEMPLES — MUDDENPORE — MAHASINGI — REVISIT BOAD—NUMBER OF VICTIMS RESCUED DURING THE SEASON—RETURN TO THE LOW COUNTRY.

CHAPTER XIII.

THE month of November, 1852, found me once more in the Sooradah infanticidal tracts, where I passed some time, and personally examined into the condition of the people. I went to five villages, and ascertained the number of children under five years of age in each family; and having thus obtained accurate information to this extent, I deputed a practised and intelligent man of my establishment to go leisurely from village to village, counting the houses and families in each, and the number of female children under five years of age in each family.

Wherever I halted, mothers with their children assembled round my tent, and I showed special favour, and made presents—handsome in their eyes—to those who had female children. To each I gave four or five yards of stout cotton cloth, and to the children strings of coloured glass beads. Combs and small looking-glasses were also distributed to laughing mothers and screaming children, who were freely admitted to my tent, which, with its contents, they examined with wonder, frequently exclaiming to each other, " It is the house of a god."

Small-pox commits great havoc throughout these hills. I endeavoured to introduce vaccination, but only with partial success; though such was the confidence entertained in our skill and desire to benefit them, that sick persons, young and old, were brought to the paths by which I was expected to pass, in the hope of receiving something to cure them.

From the infanticidal tribes I passed into the country of the sacrificing tribes of Chinna Kimedy, where I succeeded in capturing the actual perpetrators of, and several of the participators in the sacrifice that was performed last season. I was also fortunate in preventing one at the village of Bondigam, for which a victim and all necessary accessories had been hastily provided; information having enabled me to rescue the victim, a girl of about six years old, two hours only before the time appointed for her immolation. Some days after, I secured the leaders in the proposed outrage.

This had not been premeditated, but arose from a sudden temptation which these wild people could not resist. They had, some years before, paid a sum of money to a Panoo of Guddapore, to provide them with a Meriah. In the meantime came the orders prohibiting human sacrifice, and the Panoo evaded the fulfilment of his agreement. This year the Khonds were pressing, and insisted on their money being returned; the Panoo, not having the money, or, possibly, calculating that his creditors would not dare to sacrifice her, gave them his own daughter, Ootoma. But he was mistaken; the temptation was too great, the earth deity seemed to have provided the blood which had been interdicted her, and the Khonds of Bondigam at once determined on the sacrifice, which, however, I contrived to prevent.

My new assistant, Lieutenant McNeill, was successful in the western part of Chinna Kimedy, where he seized three chiefs, the joint perpetrators of a sacrifice at Solavesca of Baracooma. Fragments of the victim were brought to the Khond chiefs of Possunga, who received them; but the people afterwards came to me voluntarily in a body, ready, as they said, to endure any punishment I chose to inflict, for they had broken their pledge, and had been tempted to receive the forbidden flesh.

The ready submission of these wild men, when they could have easily evaded me, and their simple confession of wrong, clearly indicated the proper course to be pursued towards them. After impressing on their minds that the participators in Meriah flesh were equally guilty with the actual sacrificers, I dismissed them to their villages, detaining only the Khond who had brought the fragments to Possunga.

In every district there is a party sincerely disposed to abandon the sacrifice of human beings. There are also some untameable spirits, a very small minority, whom nothing but severity can restrain from their ancient murderous rite. Such persons say,

"What can he do to us?—he won't burn our villages, nor shoot us. When we threaten him he only tries to catch us, and it is our own fault if he does that." I generally did catch them, to their sorrow.

I afterwards procured the submission of the only Mootas in Chinna Kimedy that were in opposition—Toopunga and Parighur. From the latter, four Meriahs and fourteen Possiahs were delivered to me. They, being the wives originally purchased as Meriahs, and children of three of the principal chiefs of the Moota, to the very great contentment of the people, were at once restored; and I learnt that it was from fear that these cherished ones should be removed, that they were deterred from earlier making their submission, and pledging themselves, as they now did with much apparent sincerity, to forsake the custom entirely.

A very different spirit actuated the tribe of Toopunga, inhabiting a rugged country, very difficult of access. This people are a wild, unruly set; they had been long at variance with the Ooryah chief of Shoobernagery, and though summoned by us for three successive seasons, they refused to come or give up their Meriahs. They were determined to fight, and having a high character for courage among the neighbouring tribes, it was absolutely necessary for the success of my operations, endangered by this bold defiance, to bring the matter to an issue.

After a toilsome night march, I arrived early in the morning, with a small party of my Irregulars, at the principal cluster of villages of Toopunga. I endeavoured to parley with the people, but the only reply I received came in the shape of threats of destruction, and of making a Meriah of myself if I did not instantly quit their territory. Accordingly when the warriors of the tribe assembled—summoned together by the sounding of horns—they came pouring down upon me through the jungle in several parties, evidently bent on trying the question with their battle-axes. In self-defence, and much against my will, I was compelled to fire. The courage of the men of Toopunga failed, and they fled, leaving their villages (from which all property had been removed some days before) to the mercy of the excited followers of the Ooryah chief of Shoobernagery who accompanied me, and who, with the matches of their matchlock guns, set fire to three small clusters of houses.

Soon after the Khonds of Toopunga hastened to Buchadar Patur, the Ooryah chief of the district, with their Meriahs, and entreated him to intercede with me for pardon. They then made unconditional submission.

Although I regretted the attack made upon me by the people, the result had a marked and salutary effect not only on Toopunga, but on the whole of the sacrificing tribes of Chinna Kimedy. Many of the Khond chiefs expressed the greatest satisfaction at the punishment with which the audacious tribe of Toopunga had been visited, and all the Ooryah chiefs were unanimous in declaring that nothing had been wanting for the final suppression of the Meriah sacrifice but an unmistakable manifestation of the determination of the British authorities to put an end to it. They could now, they said, speak with authority to their Khonds, and point to Toopunga as a warning to those who opposed the orders of Government for the suppression of the Meriah.

From Chinna Kimedy, I proceeded to Bundari of Jeypore. I found the people anxiously looking for my arrival, uncertain as to their reception, in consequence of the sacrifice perpetrated by them last year, as already related. They soon, however, gained confidence, and came to me with their Meriahs, throwing themselves on the mercy of the Government.

Of the three victims intended for sacrifice, one had made his escape to my camp, another had died, and a third was a young woman who had undergone the usual preliminary ceremonies. Being the property of the community, they requested that she might be removed, lest her presence might prove a temptation, as they were determined to abolish the custom. Two others, young girls of twelve and fourteen, were delivered to me, with the earnest desire that they might be given in marriage to two young Khonds of the village. To this I agreed, on the usual securities being taken, and they were betrothed in my presence.

The chiefs then signed the pledge to forsake the Meriah rite, received back the grain I had caused to be removed when their village was destroyed, and a handsome present of money to assist in rebuilding it. The whole assembly admitted the justice of the punishment which had been inflicted on the people of Bundari, and wondered at the liberality and mercy of the great Government towards the penitent offenders.

Before leaving Bundari, I was requested by the chiefs to erect a post on the site of the new village they were about to build, as a mark that it was sanctioned by authority. I accordingly rode to the site of the old village, but the chiefs came in haste, exclaiming, "Not there; that ground has been accustomed for many years to human blood, and will continue to demand more—we will build on new ground." I followed where they led, and on the spot pointed out, erected a substantial post, amidst the shouts and rejoicings of men, women, and children.

From Bundari I moved to Ryabiji, where I remained several days, receiving the Khonds of the district, who came in crowds to visit me. The principal village of Ryabiji had been deserted for several years; and its inhabitants, living in small hamlets scattered around, were contemplating the building of a new Ryabiji, the old town having been abandoned, as the people told me, on account of its having been taken possession of by demons, who had brought death and disease to their families and flocks. I was solicited to mark the spot to be fixed on as the centre of the new village, which I did, and ordered a display of rockets and fireworks in the evening, to the great delight of the people, who had never seen anything of the kind before.

From the Ooryah Patur of this district, I rescued three Junnah youths, who were intended for sacrifice on the building of this village. In the presence of all the Khonds of the district, the Junnahs were delivered to me by the Patur, who in the most energetic manner abjured the rite, and called upon them to witness the abjuration, and admire the virtue of this gentleman (meaning myself), who made no distinction in administering justice between Ooryah and Khond.

From Ryabiji I marched to Godairy; and thus having passed through the strongholds of the Meriah in Jeypore, I was gratified to find that out of two hundred and twenty Khond villages, only one chief, Larunga, Maji of Dadojoringı, refused to produce his Meriahs; and he alone of all the Khonds of Jeypore performed the forbidden sacrifice last year after I had left the country.

The spectacle had been attended by a comparatively small number of people, and these were disgusted by an extra piece of barbarity, distasteful even to them. After the victims, a man and a woman, had been sacrificed, and whilst their remains were being thrown into the hole prepared for them, a child of the woman, about three years old, crept near the Maji, when the monster seized him by the legs, and, whirling him round his head, dashed him into the grave, where he was buried with the mangled remains of his mother.

It afforded me much satfsaction to see the confidence with which these wild men of Jeypore now visited my camp on this my second appearance among them, showing a remarkable contrast to their shyness of iast season; even my old opponents of Lumbargam,

Sirdapore, and Bapella, came a distance of twenty-four miles to see me.

To some of the most intelligent of the Khond chiefs I offered to restore their Meriahs for adoption, but they refused to receive them back, alleging that they would be a temptation to the people. A more convincing proof of the progress made in weaning these people from their long-cherished rite could not be desired.

At this place, my assistant joined me from the jungly villages of Lunkagher, Goomagur, and Goonjideso of Chinna Kimedy, where he was going on very successfully, when sickness compelled him to leave for a more open part of the country, bringing with him forty Meriah victims.

The inhabitants of the villages above named are a wild race known as Kootiah Khonds, speaking a dialect of the Khond language that differs considerably from that spoken by the surrounding tribes. They have very little rice cultivation, use no ploughs, and subsist chiefly on the various kinds of pulse and other dry grains grown in patches on the slopes of the hills.

From Godairy I sent the greater part of my escort, who were suffering from fever, with my assistant back to the plains through the lower part of the Chinna Kimedy Maliahs, and proceeded myself, on the 12th of January, 1853, to Bissum Cuttack of Jeypore, where I found the Khonds, under their zealous and energetic ruler, Nairraindur Deo, in perfect tranquillity and true to their pledge.

From Bissum Cuttack I pursued my course to Kalahundy of Nagpore, with the intention of visiting Tooamool, a hill principality, tributary to Kalahundy, the chief of which was under restraint at Nagpore, charged among other offences with encouraging or conniving at the performance of the Meriah sacrifice among his Khonds. I found Tooamool in such a state of anarchy, and the people so exasperated against the Rajah of Kalahundy, that it would have been worse than useless to have entered the country for the purpose of Meriah suppression. In the absence of their own chief, I should have been looked upon as a partisan of the Rajah of Kalahundy, and in that supposed character there was much risk of my being brought into collision with the Khonds and other inhabitants who were prepared to resist, as they had already done, even the authority of His Highness the Rajah of Nagpore.

I passed through a considerable portion of the Khond country of the Patna Zumindari, and satisfied myself that the prohibited rite had not, within the memory of man, existed to a greater extent than the sacrifice of one or two victims throughout the whole country once in five or six years. Patna is not a mountainous country; it has vast plains, now but partially cultivated, yet bearing the marks of former extensive cultivation in numerous remains of tanks and rice embankments.

At some distance from a village called Soorada, may be seen a remarkable collection of pagodas, which I visited, and counted one hundred and twenty of various dimensions. They were built of cut stone, without cement, and most of them are in a state of dilapidation. On the largest temple is some writing in the Devi Nigari character, but now illegible. In the centre of this group of pagodas was a circle two hundred and ten feet in circumference, surrounded by a wall of cut stone, twelve feet high, with sixty-five niches on the inner side, containing sixty figures of goddesses in a variety of attitudes; and in the centre of the circle, placed on a raised platform, sat a remarkable figure, tolerably carved, as were also the others, in stone. Few of these deities were recognised by my people, though among them were two Brahmins. The tradition here is that these temples were built by magicians, and the guide, who pointed out the way, would not go within two miles of them. Even my own people were rather uneasy. The conclusion that I came to was that this part of the country must have been occupied by a race of Hindoos, of whom there is now no trace. It is now thinly inhabited by a comparatively civilised people, who call themselves Khonds, though they do not speak their dialect. Their language and dress are Ooryah, and they are very industrious.

From Patna I passed into the small hill Zumindari of Muddenpore, tributary to Kalahundy, and found it distracted by internal dissensions, owing to a departure from the regular line of succession to the chieftainship, in the person of the youngest brother of the recently deceased chief, instead of the elder brother, who is, unhappily, a leper. Though thus disagreeing among themselves, they professed obedience to the British Government, and delivered up the last of their Meriahs.

The Rajah of Kalahundy, or Kirond, Futty Nairrain Deo, a well-educated and superior man, was with me for some days, and promised to use his best endeavours to effect a compromise between the brothers, by fixing the succession on the son of the leper, at the death of the present chief.

From Muddenpore of Kalahundy, I proceeded to Mahasingi of Chinna Kimedy, halting at several places by the way, to receive the visits of the Khonds, talk to them, settle their disputes, and make inquiries respecting the Meriah.

At Mahasingi, I met by appointment twenty-two

Ooryah and Khond chiefs of districts and villages of Chinna Kimedy, and after considerable discussion, succeeded in settling several blood feuds of long standing, some of them respecting boundaries, which I marked out. Before leaving, I strongly impressed upon the chiefs, and succeeded in convincing them, that dissensions among themselves materially weakened their authority over their people. At parting, I presented them with silver anklets and bracelets, silk, cloth, and cotton shawls, according to their rank.

These men had rendered the British Government most essential services, for several years, in their respective districts. To the cordial co-operation of the Ooryah, and the ready acquiescence of the Khond chiefs, we owe much of the success which has attended our operations. They have been put to great but unavoidable inconvenience by their attendance on my movements, and have exposed themselves to a considerable amount of obloquy for their ready assent to the views of Government. They had hitherto received no reward or remuneration beyond the usual subsistence money for themselves and followers when employed on the public service. These silver anklets and bracelets are greatly prized by the hill chiefs as marks of distinction, and it is very desirable that such people should be encouraged to continue the valuable aid they are so capable of rendering.

From Mahasingi of Chinna Kimedy I proceeded into the Boad Maliahs. Throughout, the Khonds came crowding to see their *father*, and I recognised many familiar faces among the men. They hurried on to clear the paths of jungle and other obstacles, shouting and laughing as they went.

During my stay in Boad, I learnt with great satisfaction that the Meriah sacrifice was not even spoken of among the Khonds, that the whole land had repudiated the cruel rite, and that there had not been a human victim slain since 1847. I also took the opportunity of examining a considerable portion of the road which had just been finished between Goomsur and Sohunpore on the Mahanuddy. It is difficult fully to appreciate the value of this acquisition, as a line of traffic into Nagpore, as well as to the inhabitants of Chinna Kimedy and Boad. Already was it well frequented by Brinjaries, carrying cotton and wheat to the coast. About twenty thousand bullocks have passed this season, and will return again laden with salt. The Khond inhabitants, instead of waiting in their villages for the arrival of the travelling merchants who annually visit them to purchase horns, oil seeds, turmeric, and other produce, now carry these articles to the weekly markets on the plains, obtain better prices, and purchase what they may require at more reasonable rates. I met several large parties of Khonds and Ooryahs going to the fair, and among them a good many women, who, until the opening of the road, had never ventured on the journey.

The rescued Meriah victims, settled as cultivators, are now, I am happy to say, acquiring regular habits of industry. About thirty of them were employed throughout the season in the construction of the new road.

The number of Meriahs rescued this season is one hundred and fifty, and one hundred Possiahs, or serfs, were registered and restored to their owners.

The operations were brought to a close in March, 1853, when, wearied with our labours and worn with incessant fever, which spares no one in those hills, myself and the Agency establishment returned to the low country.

CHAPTER XIV.

ALL THE TRIBES OF UPPER AND LOWER CHINNA KIMEDY VISITED—THEIR PROSPERITY AND INCREASING FAMILIARITY—PROCLAMATION—REPLY OF KHOND CHIEFS—ACT OF COURAGE OF A RESCUED VICTIM—TIGERS IN THE JUNGLE—DELIVERY OF RUNAWAY MERIAHS—CAPTURE OF A NOTORIOUS KIDNAPPER—RECEPTION AT JEYPORE—NO SACRIFICE THERE SINCE 1852—RYAGHUR AND LINKAPORE—SOME ACCOUNT OF THEM—TOOAMOOL—SICKNESS—ACCOUNT OF PEOPLE AND COUNTRY—BUNDUSIR—RAJAH FUTTY NARRAIN DEO OF KALAHUNDY—CONCLUDING REMARKS.

CHAPTER XIV.

THOUGH still suffering from the effects of fever, it was imperative that no season should pass without our presence amongst the various hill tribes. Accordingly, in November, 1853, I prepared for what proved to be my last campaign in the Khond tracts.

On my way to Chinna Kimedy I paid a short visit to the Infanticidal tribes, and was satisfied that to some extent they now rear their infant female children. The complete suppression of this practice must be the work of time and of careful supervision.

The lower and upper ranges of the Chinna Kimedy mountains were visited by myself and my assistant. We met every tribe, not one evaded us, nor was one village deserted at our approach, as in former years.

The Khonds assembled in crowds in our respective camps with a freedom never before evinced by them; selling or exchanging with our people the produce of their fields, for money, salt, bread, or pieces of cloth. No proof could be more complete or gratifying of the influence we had gained over them. After they had completed their barter, the chiefs of Mootas and villages, with their people, assembled round our tents, and listened attentively to the reading of a proclamation in the Khond dialect, reiterating the prohibition of the sacrifice of human beings, and permitting them to substitute animals instead. Copies of this proclamation were left in every district. Each chief was invited freely to express his sentiments on this proclamation, which many did without hesitation.

"When you first came among us," one stated, "we were like beasts in the jungle, doing as our fathers had done; but we now clearly comprehend that your only object in coming is to stop human sacrifice. Not a fowl or anything else has been taken from us, not even a fence injured by the people of your camp. Our fields produce crops as good as formerly, and sickness is not more prevalent. Our Meriahs have been all removed, and now we are of one mind, determined never more to have anything to do with human sacrifice. Moreover, it is no use resisting the orders of the Great Government."

In two or three places it was asked, "What are we to say to the deity?" They were told they might say whatever they pleased. Then one of the chiefs repeated the following formula: "Do not be angry with us, O goddess, for giving you the blood of beasts instead of human blood, but vent your wrath on this gentleman, who is well able to bear it. We are guiltless." Of course I had no objection to the punishment so kindly proposed for me.

Seventeen Meriahs only have been found this season in the whole of Chinna Kimedy, and these were delivered up voluntarily by their owners. Nine Meriahs who had deserted from villages on the plains, wherein they had been located, were either given up, or surrendered themselves, because their former owners would not receive them. One of these young men, on being remonstrated with, on the risk he had run of suffering a cruel and painful death, replied, "It is better to be sacrificed as a Meriah among my own people and give them pleasure, than to live on the plains. Am I not a Meriah?"

Thirty-seven Possiah women, who had been purchased when very young, were with their children (sixty-three in number) registered and restored to their husbands.

I succeeded in effecting the capture of Buddo Mundo, a notorious kidnapper of children, who last year, as already related, had given up his own daughter, Ootoma, as a Meriah. She is now, with other rescued Meriahs, under the care of the missionaries at Berhampore, and is a child of rare intelligence, and of the msot affectionate disposition.

In the Khond tracts of Jeypore my reception was most gratifying. I visited my old opponents of Lumbargam, Bapola, and Bundari, and found them contented and happy; they, with all the Khonds of Jeypore, declaring their fidelity to the pledge they had taken.

Two Meriah women who had been given in marriage to Khonds of the Sooradah Infanticidal tribes, and who had fled from their husbands, were given up, and a Meriah youth who had escaped from me last season was brought back by his owner, Indromooni Maji of Ryabiji, a fine intelligent Khond. This chief reproached me for having allowed him to escape; "for," said he, "he has undergone the ceremonies preparatory to sacrifice, and therefore is a temptation to us; take him away with you."

This, among similar instances, shews that it is not a fact, as has been stated, that "a Meriah victim once in the possession of, or produced before a Government officer, is a victim no longer; his atoning efficacy destroyed, his sacred character profaned, there is no fear after this pollution of his being sent to the stake." I have already mentioned three instances in which Meriahs were sacrificed after having been in the possession of Government officers.

Of course I took back the youth, whose name was Takoo, and settled him in one of our Meriah villages as a cultivator. He showed great pluck upon one occasion, when he was nigh losing the pair of bullocks which we gave as a little stock in trade to set up our Meriah youths. He was proceeding, as is customary, one morning to bring in the required firewood, for which purpose his yoke of bullocks was necessary; and it so happened that on this day he joined a lot of Ooryahs of the low country, who were bent on a similar errand. They had only proceeded a short distance, when a tiger sprang suddenly out of the jungle, and seized the near bullock belonging to Takoo. At the sight of the beast, the Ooryahs, without a single exception, fled in the wildest alarm; but Takoo, in presence of the tiger, deliberately walked round to the off bullock, cut with his axe the rope that secured him to the yoke and to his now bleeding mate, and having thus gallantly released him, he brought him safe home. Such brave conduct deserved and received a suitable reward.

There has been no sacrifice, nor attempt to sacrifice, in Jeypore since March, 1852.

From Jeypore I passed in a north-westerly direction through the Zumindaries of Ryaghur and Linkapore, a fine, open, level country, and well cultivated. The population consists of Khonds and Tellogoos. The Khonds are an industrious and civilised race, and pay rent for their land like their Tellogoo neighbours.

They acknowledged having occasionally procured the flesh of a victim from Jeypore, but assured me that for many years no sacrifice had taken place among themselves. Through these Zumindaries upwards of twenty thousand Brinjary bullocks pass from the interior to the coast with oil seeds, wheat, and cotton, and return laden with salt.

From Linkapore I sent my assistant through the hilly country of Bundasir of Kalahundy, inhabited by sacrificing tribes of Khonds, while I turned nearly west towards Tooamool. Sickness had for some days been on the increase in my camp, and at the second march into the mountain ranges of Tooamool, I had scarcely a man for service. The doctor in medical charge of the camp, and the officer commanding my escort of sepoys, being added to the list with severe fever, I was compelled—while it was yet possible to procure carriage for the sick—to send them all back to the low country, where I am glad to say they arrived in safety. I continued my tour with my own Irregulars or Sebundies. One of this gallant little body, and one, too, of the few Khonds whom I could induce to enter this service, and to put on uniform, was killed by a tiger, in singular coincidence with his own presentiment. He was on the hills with Lieutenant McNeill, and joined in repelling the attack made by the Khonds on that officer's camp at Oorladoney, where two or three of the assailants were shot. This man became strongly imbued with the idea that one of the Khonds then killed was possessed of the power of the "Phulto Bag," and would certainly destroy him and all his family. Nothing could shake his belief in the destiny which he was convinced awaited him and his.

On returning to the low country he begged for leave to visit his home on the hills, where his family were settled. Previous to his departure, in a very serious manner he requested that his uniform might be taken charge of, as he felt convinced that he should never live to return to his duty. He arrived safely at his native village, and all went well for a brief period, when most singularly it happened that whilst watching some cattle at night, as is their custom on the hills, this poor fellow was seized by a tiger and cruelly mutilated. He shortly afterwards died from the effect of his wounds; but before he expired he said that he was one of those who had fired at and killed a Khond at Oorladoney, that this Khond had assumed the form of a tiger, and so avenged himself.

It would have required a miracle to have persuaded his friends that his fate was but a strange coincidence.

Tooamool, which we reached by a succession of difficult ghats, is on the table-land of a high range of mountains, in length about thirty-two miles east and west, and in breadth about fourteen. The climate is very trying; the thermometer in my tent at six o'clock in the morning ranged from 35 deg. to 38 deg., and at noon from 81 deg. to 83 deg.; we had often hoar frost and thin ice, which was there seen for the first time by my native followers.

The inhabitants subsist on different kinds of maize, grown on the slopes of their hills, which are almost cleared of jungle, and cultivated to the top. Their rice cultivation is very scanty. The crops this season had failed in these high regions, as well as in the plains, so I had great difficulty in supplying even my reduced camp, and we were frequently on half rations.

I found the Khonds tractable and well disposed, though at first somewhat alarmed, but they soon gained confidence, and men, women, and children came into my camp freely. They had never seen a European before, and my tent and its contents, together with the elephants and horses in camp, were great attractions.

I ascertained beyond a doubt that the Khonds of Tooamool did not rear Meriahs, but when they had determined on a sacrifice, they applied to the Tat Rajah, who sold to them some unfortunate person accused of sorcery, for sums varying from twenty to fifty rupees.

After the usual meetings and consultations, and frequent palavers amongst the chiefs, they, in the presence of their people, signed the pledge to forsake the Meriah rite for ever. They declared that no sacrifice had taken place since the removal of their Tat Rajah, three years ago, to Nagpore, where he lately died a prisoner.

"They had heard," they said, "that the 'Company'"—they knew the mysterious name—"had sent a great officer to the Khonds of Jeypore and Chinna Kimedy to abolish the Meriah sacrifice, and had felt disappointed that no officer had been sent to them. They were now, however, pleased to find that they were held in equal estimation with their brethren of other countries."

At Koorlapaut, a tributary of Kalahundy, on the same mountain range as Tooamool, the Khonds came to me with perfect confidence. They made a statement, with respect to the Meriah, similar to that given by the Khonds of Tooamool.

My assistant, who traversed the Khond mountains of Bundasir of Kalahundy, found the Khonds most submissive and tractable. Formerly, when they required a sacrifice, they purchased a victim from some distant country; but the Rajah of Kalahundy, Futty Narrain Deo, having forbidden the Meriah, and twice punished them very severely, once for sacrificing, and a second time for attempting to sacrifice, they were resolved to give it up; and now that the great

Government had sent an officer to them, they were confirmed in that resolution. In plain fact, they knew, from the experience of their neighbours, that no opposition of theirs was likely to be effective.

To this Rajah, Futty Narrain Deo, great credit is due, for his earnest and effectual efforts for the suppression of human sacrifices in the Hill Zumindaries under his authority; and all that was required to perfect his work was the personal communication which I have now had with his Khonds. I impressed them with the wholesome conviction that not only were they responsible to their Rajah, but also to the Government, whose officers had penetrated into all their fastnesses.

In Kalahundy I met several large droves of Brinjary bullocks proceeding to the coast for salt; their owners complained bitterly of the heavy transit-dues levied from them by the different petty Zumindars, or landed proprietors, through whose territory they passed, amounting in the aggregate to nearly half the price paid by them at the sea-coast for their salt. The Zumindars keep the paths by which the cattle travel tolerably clear, and protect the Brinjaries from molestation, though they are well able to take care of themselves.

Could the population which has been driven away by famine and disease be replaced, the vast plains of

Kalahundy and Lower Patna, now lying waste, studded with ancient temples and ruined tanks, might become as rich and productive in cotton and other crops as the most fertile parts of Nagpore.

The narrative of the operations which brought to a close this season's labour, speaks for itself. The Khonds everywhere were making sure and certain progress in their complete emancipation from the cruel rite of human sacrifices which for ages had prevailed amongst them.

It was destined that my humble but earnest labours amongst the mountain tribes of Khondistan should this season terminate for ever; but I can never cease to feel the warmest and most heartfelt interest in their welfare. My work in these hills was always to me a labour of love, and I linger with affectionate remembrance on the many years I lived among the rude tribes, and pitched my tent in their mountain villages.

CHAPTER XV.

NATIVE COUNCILS AND DEBATES RESPECTING THE ABOLITION OF THE MERIAH SACRIFICE—OPINIONS OF CAPTAIN HILL RESPECTING THEIR RAJAHS—THEIR MINISTERS—MY EFFORTS TO SECURE THEIR CO-OPERATION—CEREMONIOUS VISITS — PROCEEDINGS OF THE DURBAR—OORYAH CHIEFS—MY ATTEMPTS TO CONCILIATE THEM—LOYALTY OF NARRAINDUR DEO—REPORT OF MR. STUBBINS—VILLAGES ESTABLISHED BY ME—CAPTAIN M'NEILL'S ACCOUNT OF THEM—NUMBER OF RESCUED VICTIMS—HOW THEY WERE DISPOSED OF—LIBERALITY OF THE GOVERNMENT—I LEAVE INDIA.

CHAPTER XV.

It will not, I trust, be concluded from the foregoing imperfect narrative that the hill tribes, more especially in the days of our earliest intercourse with them, readily yielded to our wishes, and abandoned their ancient rite. Such a conclusion would be very far from the fact, but I have not deemed it requisite to exhaust the reader's patience with details of the almost interminable discussions by day and by night which invariably preceded any surrender on their part. These wearying debates were an absolute necessity, and one of the conditions of success, but to have described every council as it was held would have rendered this account intolerably prolix.

I always took care that they should know what was the sole purpose of our visit. It was not possible always to conduct our operations in the same way. Our plans varied according to ever-changing circumstances, and the necessities induced by such changes.

Sometimes the people were stolid, apathetic, and listless; at others, excited, passionate, and senseless. I found it absolutely necessary to be prepared for all they might say or do. Moderation and resolution combined, finally conquered our most determined opponents. Upon all occasions I took very good care that they should clearly learn the feelings with which we regarded their detestable custom.

It should, however, be remembered that this race, if not entitled fully to the name of savage, is still on the very lowest verge of civilization, and could not therefore be expected to embrace or comprehend reasoning adapted to a people of more cultivated understanding.

Captain Hill, who spent some time in the Orissa chain of mountains, very justly observed that the disposition of the Khond partook much of animal suspicion and cunning, and that the varying ideas of his mind were more nearly allied to instinct than to the powers of reasoning, and perception between right and wrong, which are the results of education and civilization. It must also be recollected that the Khond is of a suspicious nature; especially so are those who have grown grey in their traditions; they always fancy you are endeavouring to entrap them, or to compromise them in some shape, and are very slow to believe that there is not some plot against their lives and happiness, hidden under the cloak of an attempt to suppress human sacrifices.

These old men had little to look for in the future; they earnestly desired to die as they had lived, and for them hope had fewer charms than reminiscence. Hence they clung as steadfastly as they could to their superstition, but it was always my aim to wrest from them all hope in respect of the continuance of Meriah sacrifice, with its mournful and miserable details. I impressed upon them the necessity of abandoning their barbarous practice, and by careful supervision and constant visits I kept alive in their minds the feeling of that necessity.

But preparatory to any discussion with the Khond tribes, there were two highly essential preliminaries to fulfil, without which my mission would have been perilled. The rulers or rajahs of the low country, and the chiefs of the high lands, must first be won over to our views. I will add here a few words on the position held by these two distinct classes in respect of the Khonds. First, the Rajahs.

It is almost impossible to define with accuracy the relative position of Khond and Rajah. It is far too vague and indeterminate to be clearly expressed. It is quite certain that the latter claims an obedience which the former never yields, whilst it is no less certain that the one had a very strong and, as we should call it, loyal feeling towards the other. It must be allowed that generally, and with singular good judgment, the Rajahs have interfered with their hill subjects as little as possible. There are certain perquisites, fines, and forfeits which are in reality due to the chief; but in truth, it always depends upon the temper of the Khonds at the time whether they pay anything or nothing.

Whenever the Rajah deputes one of his officers or ministers to pay the Khonds a visit, such functionary is received with great honour, as a general rule, and presents of rice, vegetables, &c., are bestowed upon him; but the people assert that all this is purely complimentary, and could not be exacted as a matter of right. Indeed, nearly all the tribes profess to regard themselves as completely independent; they pay no rent or taxes, and believe themselves to be the original owners of the soil. Amongst themselves they sometimes sell or rent their fields—a matter very fertile of disputes, where there exists no possible means of registering or in any way recording their contracts. Much of my time was spent in arranging these difficulties.

Notwithstanding, however, this very vague allegiance, my first step, as I have already said, was always directed to secure the cordial co-operation of the Rajahs of the plains. This process was not very difficult, but it was very tedious. These men, or rather their ministers—for in general the Rajah is a mere puppet in leading strings—are governed by self-interest; and when they found that they would be no losers by affording us their influence, limited though it was, to attain our objects with their hill subjects, that influence was enlisted on our side. Presents to the Rajah and his subordinates, and the tedious formality of a visit, added to a conciliatory demeanour, were the chief means I employed to achieve my end.

The state visit of one of these little magnates is a most tedious affair, they being enormous sticklers for etiquette. When the day of visitation (and a heavy one it is) is fixed, it becomes imperative to ascertain with accuracy the rank and names of all the relatives, ministers, and followers the Rajah means to bring with him, to the end that, their precedence being duly established, they may all be ranged at the audience in accordance with custom and their respective ranks.

Some of the dignitaries are honoured with a chair, some sit on a carpet, and the great mass of followers remain standing, but all must have a place assigned, or offence is taken.

The Rajah fixes the hour of his visit, and as these gentlemen set no value on that precious article, time, I was frequently kept waiting with my whole establishment, and the troops requisite to form a guard of honour, for three or four hours. After our patience had been thus strained, the discordant sounds of native music, the shrill blowing of pipes, and the heavy beating of drums, announced that the Rajah was in motion for my camp. Gradually the procession, consisting of all the elephants the dark potentate possessed, or could borrow, all the troops, horse and foot, that he could muster, and a rabble innumerable, approached the durbar, or audience tent.

On descending from his elephant, or alighting from his palankeen, as the case might be, the Rajah generally fell, as it were, into the arms of two men stationed for that purpose, and leaning on these supports, he tottered towards my tent. Not that he was unable to walk without aid, but this elegant fiction represented his greatness, and the vast affairs of his little empire, which literally weighed him to the ground! This always produced a certain effect upon the minds of the immense mob present. I say immense, because on these occasions the whole country turns out.

I meet his Highness at the door of the tent and receive a small offering, generally of money, in token of the submission he owes the paramount power in India, whose representative for the time I am. I then conduct him to a seat prepared opposite to my own; his relatives, ministers, &c., follow, and all occupy the places assigned them; the rabble press in on all sides, and it is in vain the guards attempt to drive them back, they *will* thrust themselves into the unoccupied space in the tent. The atmosphere becomes suffocating; the reeking odour from this dense mass of dark humanity being far less fragrant than Rimmel's perfumed fountains.

When order and silence are in some degree restored, I ask in a tender tone if his Highness is in the enjoyment of good health.

To which he somewhat evasively replies, "I trust the protector and cherisher of the poor [meaning myself] is very well."

I bow, the Rajah bows, and there our conversation begins—and ends. Everybody then looks at everybody else, and this silly, unmeaning, and most tiresome farce is kept up for half an hour, when I gently rise, which is the signal that the Durbar is over.

I now conduct the Rajah to the door, embrace and take leave of him. He falls again into the arms of his attendants, whilst a man with a huge gold stick bawls forth all his titles and honours, that no one may be ignorant that they are in the presence of so much greatness. Oriental court etiquette permits no business or business communication on the first or state visit.

This purgatorial infliction was part of the price I

had to pay for the co-operation of these gentlemen.

However useful the assent and good will of the Rajahs, it was a far more important step to conciliate and win to our purposes the Hill or Ooryah chiefs, called, by the Khonds, Bissois or Paturs, according to the district in which they dwelt. It was my fate to deal with sixty-five of these chiefs, and although we often quarrelled, and sometimes I had to deal shortly and sharply with them personally, it affords me ummixed satisfaction to be able to assert that I never removed one of them from the office he held ; on the contrary, I used all my influence to strengthen their position in the eyes of their Khonds.

It appeared evident to me that I should only be sowing the seeds of anarchy and confusion if I attempted to subvert the authority of the men who enjoyed the entire confidence of the Khond population. It could not be reasonably expected that I should find them all equally well disposed to forward my views, or that they should at first exhibit any great zeal to serve me. They cared nothing themselves about the Meriah rite, but they approved of it because they benefited by it, and received from the Khonds certain perquisites every time a sacrifice was offered. It was not surprising, then, that at first they received my overtures coldly, and resorted not unfrequently to intrigue to thwart me.

I was not, however, to be easily baffled, and as I was generally made acquainted with the devices they were preparing to get rid of or deceive me, I contrived to render them nugatory, and strove, by forbearance and conciliation, to make a proper impression on their hearts. I went out shooting with them, talked often, and in the friendliest way, to them, made them presents of what they most wanted, prescribed for their ailments, and gave medicine if they were sick; smoked with them, was kind to their children, and in short left no stone unturned to win their friendship and adherence to our cause.

At last I succeeded, and the time was well spent, for without their assistance I should have been almost helpless. It was expedient, therefore, to endure much rather than jeopardise the work I had to do by offending such men.

Often they would keep me waiting for days together, and endeavour, by all kinds of lying excuses, to evade coming near me; but I patiently submitted to all this, knowing the surpassing advantages I should ultimately derive from their support. Without these chiefs, who, from hereditary sway, were much loved and venerated by their several tribes, I should have had almost insurmountable difficulty in getting myself into personal communication with the Khonds themselves. It was half the battle to gain an interview;

when that was accomplished the foundation of a successful campaign was laid.

Again, no one could explain so well the true object of my coming amongst them. They could, if they chose, at any moment, have incited a warlike race to take up arms against me; or, on the other hand, they could smooth the way for what I wanted, and prepare their Khonds to meet and hear me in a friendly spirit —so potent were they for good or evil.

It will at once be seen, then, that the services of these Ooryah chiefs were invaluable, and that they were the principal instruments I employed in the suppression of the Meriah rite. On them, too, I chiefly depend for maintaining the ground we have gained.

An instance I will mention of the hearty co-operation of one of them, Narraindur Deo, of Bissum Cuttack. He had been won over to our side, and was our warm ally. A sacrifice was proclaimed to take place in Jeypore, in March, 1852. It came to Narraindur Deo's knowledge that a party of his Khonds intended to cross their frontier—for Jeypore is some distance from Bissum Cuttack—and participate in the Meriah festival. He acted most energetically; summoned his Khonds, reminded them of their pledge to me, and of the disgrace they would incur by a violation of it; forbade them going, in the most peremptory manner, and vowed, if they disobeyed him, that he would waylay them on their return, and shoot every man he found. This threat was sufficient—not one Khond went to the place of sacrifice.

In other instances, purposed attacks on me were averted by their interference ; and in those onslaughts on my camp I have narrated, and which I was obliged to repel, the Ooryah chiefs coming in afterwards as intercessors for the discomfited Khonds, acquired new influence, and the submission which followed was complete.

I have been desirous to be as brief as possible, yet am anxious that the system I pursued, dating so far back as 1837, should be clearly understood, as I had to grapple with a gigantic evil. No subsidiary measures were neglected, no advantages that we could properly bestow upon the people were left unconferred ; aided by the elders of the tribes, justice was administered, and many an ancient feud, as I have described, definitively healed. All these were admirable auxiliaries, but the reader will, I trust, have perceived that the keystone of the system was the conquest of the Ooryah chiefs, without whose aid and co-operation it would have been as easy to have built a city in the air as to have suppressed human sacrifices amongst the Khonds.

I anticipate the best results from the diffusion of knowledge and the spread of education in the Orissa hills, by means of the rescued Meriah victims undergoing a course of instruction in the plains.

I placed about two hundred of the Meriah children in the mission-schools of the low country. The great object I had in view was that the most intelligent might be brought up as teachers, and eventually settle in their native hills, where, by precept and example, under God's blessing, they might be instrumental in winning some of their own wild people to the pure principles of our holy religion. It was a well understood part of their education that they should not be allowed to forget the Khond language, but that it should be cultivated by means of the educational works prepared in that dialect by Captain Frye.

The Government of India, on my recommendation, made a very liberal provision for all the Meriahs, whether young or old. Some of the children were confided to the care of Mr. and Mrs. Stubbins, and Mr. and Mrs. Wilkinson, who resided at the military station of Berhampore, in Ganjam. Others were sent to Mr. and Mrs. Buckley, at Cuttack, in the province of that name, and to Mr. Bachelor, an American missionary at Balasore. I had every reason to be well satisfied with the training bestowed by these worthy people upon the Meriah children, and the attachment that sprang up between the teachers and taught was sincere and lasting. I often visited them, and observed, with heartfelt pleasure, their neat and clean appearance, their orderly behaviour, and their progress in learning.

When the boys and girls were sufficiently old to enter the married state, and when their education was completed, partners were selected from the different schools, and the unions solemnised. I gave each couple a marriage dowry to start them in life, and they were well assured that the same care and solicitude for their welfare which had attended them since they had been in our hands would not fail them in the future.

It may interest those who read this book to peruse the following out of very many similar notes I received on the occasion of the marriage of a Meriah couple. It is from Mrs. Stubbins:

"Berhampore, November 3rd.

"My dear Colonel Campbell,

"Rachel and Daniel (two rescued victims) were married yesterday, and leave for the hills early to-morrow morning. Rachel has been such a good obedient girl, that I really feel sorry to part with her. I rejoice, however, in the thought that she is a true believer in Christ, and hope she may be able to act consistently in her new position. I should not be surprised if she should at first feel the loneliness of her situation. To obviate this difficulty as much as possible, I have given her a supply of knitting and crochet materials, and she is very much pleased with the thought of working for you. Amongst other things, she purposes making some socks for your little grandson, and in due time I daresay there will be an opportunity of forwarding them to you. Our best wishes and prayers will follow this young couple, and most sincerely do we hope they may be made a blessing to the natives by whom they are surrounded.

"I trust your valuable life and health may be preserved, and that you may continue to have good news from your dear children.

"Yours very sincerely,

"E. STUBBINS."

I need not dwell longer on the fate and fortunes of our wards; they were trained to various occupations—teachers, artificers, or husbandmen, according to the bent of their inclination. The majority decided to follow the plough and till the soil. I obtained, therefore, several grants of land, usually uncleared forest, from Government; and established villages, where, to this hour, the Meriahs live in happiness and comfort.

Captain McNeill, who long and ably laboured

amongst the Khonds, took peculiar interest in these villages, and only left them about ten months ago. An engineer himself of no mean skill, he was enabled to show them new and improved methods of irrigating their lands, and a greater boon could not have been conferred upon them. I am sure these Meriah villagers will deeply feel the loss of their tried friend and protector, Captain McNeill, but the supreme Government considered last year that the time had arrived when the work of Meriah suppression had been so completely accomplished, that no further special agency was required, and the whole Khond country reverted to its former masters.

I daresay the Government arrived at a sound conclusion, and certainly none of the officers of the late agency will demur to a resolution which contains so flattering a compliment to their own success; but I earnestly trust that the new authorities will carefully study the character of the people entrusted to their charge, and not seek to force them within the pale of a moral or judicial code for which at present they are quite unfitted. They have nobly kept their pledge to us, in abstaining from sacrifice; we must keep ours to them, in not seeking to impose on them vexatious regulations or unjust taxes.

The total number of Meriahs rescued during the operations I have endeavoured to sketch, from 1837 to 1854, was one thousand five hundred and six; and the following are the countries from which they were taken:—

	Males	Females.	Total.
From Goomsur	101	122	223
„ Boad	181	164	345
„ Chinna Kimedy	313	353	666
„ Jeypore	77	116	193
„ Kalahundy	43	34	77
„ Patna	2	„	2
	717	789	1,506

And within the same period, eleven hundred and fifty-four Possiahs were registered and restored to their owners.

The next record will show how these fifteen hundred and six Meriahs have been provided for:—

	Males.	Females.	Total.
Restored to relatives and friends, or given for adoption to persons of character in the plains	194	148	342
Given in marriage to Khonds and others of suitable condition . , .	„	267	267
Supporting themselves in public or private service	53	22	75
Died	69	88	157
Deserted	63	14	77
In Missionary schools at Cuttack, Berhampore, and Balasore . . .	116	84	200
Settled as cultivators in different villages	195	111	306
At the Asylum, Sooradah . . .	27	55	82
	717	789	1,506

Among the infanticidal tribes great progress has been made in weaning them from their cruel practice.

The result of the inquiry of 1854 shows a registry of nine hundred and one females under five years of age, in 2,149 families located in villages, where I can state from my own observation that in 1848 there were few, if any, female children to be seen.

I have very frequently been asked if I could with any accuracy state the number of human beings annually sacrificed previous to the interference of the British Government. I never could obtain precise or satisfactory information on this point. The Khonds always betrayed a marked unwillingness to speak on the subject, and what evidence they ever did give was always most conflicting. In 1837, Mr. Ricketts, the commissioner in Cuttack, rescued sixteen boys and eight girls from the Boad district; and in his report to the Government he states that one Khond told him he had witnessed fifty sacrifices; whilst another said he had never seen more than three or four. I presume both these men spoke of all the sacrifices they had seen in their lives.

Again in February, 1846, Captain McPherson writes, that about one hundred victims had been immolated in the tracts of Boad, bordering upon Goomsur, in anticipation of the usual season for sacrifice, and his approximate estimate of Meriahs sacrificed is five hundred annually, and that the victims are counted by thousands. And lastly, it is mentioned in one of Captain Hill's letters, that in Bustar the practice prevailed to an enormous extent, and that, upon one occasion alone, twenty-five or twenty-seven full grown men were immolated, and this was called the great sacrifice.

My own impression, founded on much experience in these hills, is, that generally the reports were exaggerated; few Khond districts were free from the stain of human sacrifice, but the very great expense attendant upon procuring the victims and performing the connected ceremonies, tended in a certain degree to limit the number slain. Each cluster of villages would most probably celebrate a sacrifice annually, and if special causes rendered it necessary, extra victims might be offered; but I think I shall not be very far wrong in estimating the annual number at one hundred and fifty.

Be this as it may, we can now, thank God, look back upon such atrocities as a thing of the past. It affords me intense gratification to be able to give so satisfactory a statement of the success of my measures for the entire and complete abandonment of this cruel custom.

I should be committing an act of great injustice towards the Government of India, whose support I uniformly enjoyed, were I to conclude this work without acknowledging the liberal spirit in which they received every proposition I made on behalf of my mission. Any amount of money I asked for was ungrudgingly sanctioned, and the warmest marks of approval were bestowed upon my humble but earnest endeavours to give effect to their benevolent intentions. I often encountered opposition, and the press never ceased to attack myself and my measures; but up to the moment of resigning my most interesting and important charge into the hands of others, I was encouraged and supported by the liberal conduct of the Government; a few of whose approving testimonies, which I have thought might not be uninteresting, will be found in the Appendix.

Warned by increasing ill-health that I must seek relaxation in another clime, I handed over my charge, in March, 1854, to Captain Macviccar, who had rejoined me from England, and was prepared to take my placc.

CHAPTER XVI.

RECENT GEOLOGICAL SURVEY OF INDIA—THE COAST OF ORISSA—CHILKA LAKE — ARRANGEMENT OF THE BEDS—ALLEGED DISCOVERIES OF COAL AND IRON—ALLUVIAL PLAIN—HILLS—JUNGLE—RARE MINERALS—TALCHEER AND ATURGH BASINS—SANDSTONE SERIES—CARBONIFEROUS SERIES—UPPER GRIT—RIVER GOLD—BUILDING MATERIALS—REPORT OF LIEUTENANT RIGBY ON THE STONE AND TIMBER OF THE COUNTRY—MANUFACTURE OF SALT—RICE—VEGETATION AND CHARACTER OF THE FLORA—OIL PRODUCING PLANTS—SUGAR CANE —TOBACCO—ABUNDANCE OF FISH.

CHAPTER XVI.

WITH the preceding chapter this volume might very properly have concluded, and certainly would have done so if I had consulted only my own feelings. But I have been urgently requested to add an account of the natural resources of Orissa, and some geographical and geological description of the province. From the excellent memoir published by the Superintendent of the Geological Survey in 1859, under the auspices of the Governor-General of India, I am enabled to furnish valuable and reliable data for a geological description; I am, therefore, indebted to Dr. Oldham for much of what follows.

In Mr. Stirling's history there are only meagre references to these subjects; and although other reports, professing to contain scientific information, have, from time to time, within the last twenty years, been submitted to the Government of India, it does not appear that the able conductor of the survey thought any of them of value, as, in his introductory memoir, he refers, and that but very briefly, to only one of them.

There has been no government survey of the coast of Orissa, a want which has been pointed out by the Royal Geographical Society in one of their recent annual reports; but there is a description of the appearance of that part of the Bay of Bengal which washes its shores, in the Geological Survey I have just named, that leaves little to be desired respecting the coast line. Orissa is seen to project some miles, arising from the fluviatile deposits encroaching on the sea. In the extreme south of the province there exists a well-marked indentation in the hills, that at a distant period was a bay; but the deposits, in conjunction with a spit of sand from the hills near Ganjam, have nearly closed in a volume of sea water forty miles long, by twelve wide, communicating with the sea by means of a small channel, gradually decreasing. This water is Chilka Lake.

The ground rises beyond into detached peaks and ranges of low hills, generally separated by alluvial plains, upon which the laterite, a deposit I shall presently describe, rises to a considerable height. This region must have been originally the bed of a sea containing islands of gneiss, varying in size and elevation. Sandstone prevails in the hills ranging to the west and south-west of the town of Cuttack.

These have not been affected by the influence of sea water, that has thinned the rocks of Bankee, Khoordah, and the immediate districts; which renders it probable that the deposit of the metamorphic rock succeeded the denudation.

Gneiss and quartz, with intrusive trap and syenite; sandstone, laterite, older alluvium and alluvium of the river deltas and blown sands, form the ordinary arrangement of the beds in Orissa, which territory includes the districts of Pooree, Cuttack, and Balasore, explored in 1857-8 by Messrs. W. T. Blanford and Harry Child. This, with Midnapore on the north, and Bancoorah, a neighbouring province, that was surveyed in the same season, form an area of fourteen thousand square miles.

Mr. Stirling had nearly fifty years before declared that the granite rose from about three hundred to two thousand feet, generally red in tint, containing veins of red and white soap-stone, and particles of imperfectly formed garnets; but that decomposition and disintegration have frequently changed the texture of the rock into sandstone and slate, the same agency having also produced a soil which covers every hill with vegetation. At their base, he stated, is usually the iron-clay, in beds of considerable thickness.

Rocks of a fine white granite, according to his description, are met with, containing hornblende and mica; and are intersected by veins of trap, a green stone of a basaltic character. Talc and mica slate, and schistose chlorites, passing into serpentine, too, are, he says, abundant. He declares, also, that limestone, in calcareous nodules, may be found both in the hills and plains.

A good deal of attention has been paid to the subject, in consequence of the repeated reports to Government of alleged coal and iron districts of great value. In 1837, Lieutenant Kittoe announced a discovery of beds of coal, and of iron mines, but when sent in search of these treasures, he came back to Calcutta empty-handed. In 1842, an engineer officer, Lieutenant Rigby, reported a variety of building materials, and produced specimens worthy of consideration. Surveys were ordered of the coal districts, but the result was eminently unsatisfactory. The coal turned out either to be a non-combustible shale, or the seam was so thin, or lay so deep, as not to be worth working.*

Of the other product there is a better account, for the Talcheer iron has long been in repute in India for its excellent quality. Mr. Blanford states that the ore found in the Damoodah beds of the Talcheer

* "Preliminary Notice on the Coal and Iron of Talcheer in the Tributary Maliahs of Cuttack." By Thomas Oldham, LL.D., &c. "Memoirs of the Geological Surveys of India." Vol. i.

coal-field is rich in metal, and that abundance of it is to be found throughout the district, close to the surface. The native process of producing the metal is very defective; the charcoal from the *sàl*, an Indian tree, *Shorea robusta*, being extravagantly used, and the machinery of the simplest construction.

In the course of his able Memoir, Dr. Oldham suggests a plan for obtaining from the country its metallic resources, at the expense of the surrounding forest; by clearing a circuit of twenty miles, he expects to be able to produce 24,000 tons of iron annually. Such calculations may not be quite trustworthy, but there is no doubt of the existence of the two principal elements on which they are founded—the prodigious extent of the jungle, and the richness and abundance of the ore. Of the latter, one specimen from Kunkerie yielded 46.8 per cent., and another from Taleyra forty-seven per cent. of metallic iron.

Though the coal-fields are less valuable, they possess many features of interest that have been well detailed in another Memoir, written by Messrs. Blanford and Theobald (in the same volume of the Survey), whose description of the surrounding district will well repay perusal. The country explored in the years 1855-6 is that between the Brahmini and Mahanuddy rivers, from the western boundary of the so-called Talcheer coal-fields, 84 deg., 20 min., east longitude, to a few miles east of Cuttack.

A cultivated alluvial plain, in breadth from fifteen to forty-five miles, stretches from the coast to the foot of the hills, which rise separately to the north of Cuttack, are of inconsiderable size, though steep, suggesting, say the surveyors, in connection with the ridges and bosses spread over the surrounding country, the idea of an upraised archipelago. In truth, it seems probable that the ocean waters of the western bay of Bengal at one time swept the entire country, and Messrs. Blanford and Theobald assure us that a small sinking of the land would cause it now to be submerged in the same manner.

The hills of greater elevation start up in rugged ridges from ten to fifteen miles long, and from east to west; those of greatest length being to the west of Ungool are generally well rounded, and covered with jungle, while those formed of sandstone sediment are flat at top, formed in steep ridges, having valleys between, and show a fluvial rather than a marine action. At Rehrakōl they are thickly wooded; to the west they attain a higher elevation, and are more numerous, rising at Rann Hill, in Rampur, to two thousand two hundred feet. Hill and plain being generally a dense jungle, the haunts of savage animals, including the tiger, leopard, hyena, and bear, with the bison, hog, and several species of deer.

Indeed, the thickness of this forest presents great obstacles to a careful survey; nevertheless the evidence is clear that the land is composed of metamorphic rocks, with occasional dykes and veins of igneous origin, and basins of sedimentary deposits —the whole tract of ground between the so-called coal-fields, and also the hills of the district, consisting essentially of different varieties of gneiss, covered in the low coast country, and in the river deltas, by alluvium.*

The rocks are of four kinds—igneous, metamorphic, sedimentary, and what the surveyors call chemico-aqueous. The first are mostly granite of a dioritic character, the dykes and veins being composed nearly of pure quartz and felspar—two kinds of the latter—and possess large crystals of mica and quartz. The dykes are narrow—from four inches to two feet broad—the smallest being very numerous, and contain a variety of granite, disclosing large crystals of black tourmaline, in veins from one to two feet thick, as may be observed in the bed of the Brahmini, near Kamlong, in a nullah near Gotiapol, and close to Ramidi. In this neighbourhood the surveyor found, in addition to the schorl crystals, which were some-

* "Geological Survey of India," i., 35.

times an inch and a half in diameter, crystals of apetite, beryl, or a pseudo-morph of that mineral, and a transparent yellow mineral, probably chrysoberyl. Large crystals of adularia felspar, quartz, and honey-coloured mica are also to be met with ; while in the bed of a water-course that crosses the Ungool and Cuttack road, near Raseil, there is a granite vein, containing crystals of Zircon as well as a black mineral, considered to be titaniferous iron pegmatite, that is found in the gneiss westward of the coal-field near Ampul. The granite is older than the sedimentary rocks, and the granitic veins contemporaneous with the metamorphism of the gneiss.

Dykes of a hard green rock, composed, apparently, of quartz and hornblende, pass through the gneiss at various points near the south-east boundary of the Talcheer field, at Sakuasinga and near Ramidi. They are of greater age than the carboniferous strata.

The metamorphic rocks consist of micaceous and quartzose gneiss, as well as gneiss in which the mica is changed to hornblende; this variety being highly crystalline, approaching in character to actenilite. One rock, which largely prevails, is almost a pure quartz. There is also micaceous gneiss in every variety, from an apparently perfect granite.

Hornblende schilt occurs at the junction of the Teugrin nullah with the river Brahmini, disclosing well-defined crystals of actenilite. The gneiss assumes so closely the aspect of granite, as to be readily mistaken for it—as it was by Mr. Stirling. Examples are described as existing near Kokodong, where large bosses of apparently highly porphyritic gneiss, contain disseminated garnets and imperfect crystals of adularia felspar.*

The influence of rapid currents of water, and subsequent weathering, is evident upon the surface of some of these rocks, giving to the rounded hummocks much of the appearance of glacial action, as seen in the *Roches Moutonnées.*

The Talcheer basin contributes the bulk of the sedimentary rocks, which are sandstones, conglomerates, and carbonaceous shales, wfth laterite and a few other superficial deposits. This is situated about fifty miles to the north-west of Cuttack, and contains nearly the whole of the territory of the Rajah of that district, as well as portions of Deukenāl, Bamrah, Rampur, Rehrakōl and Ungool, which has become a British possession, being about seventy miles long, and from fifteen to twenty broad. These rocks occur sparingly in the Atgurh basin, which exists close to Cuttack, and extends twenty miles westward, up the Mahanuddy. The beds here are generally of great thickness, the Mahadewa group of upper grit being

* "Geological Survey of India," i., 41.

estimated at from fifteen hundred to two thousand feet; the Damoodah, or carboniferous shale, at nearly eighteen hundred feet; and the Talcheer, or lower sandstone, at from five hundred to six hundred feet. This is but an approximate calculation—the aggregate thickness is believed to be much greater.

The lower sandstone series comprise, in ascending order, a boulder-bed, fine sandstone, designated as tesselated, and blue nodular shale. They are met with, extending westward, about twenty miles from the Brahmini. The lowest looks like a conglomerate of granite and gneiss fragments, as seen near Purongo, in a matrix of dark green silt; elsewhere, the bed varies from a coarse sandstone to a fine shale. In place of this a remarkably coarse sandstone sometimes rests on the gneiss.

The "tesselated" is a fine-grained compact stone, of a pale-yellow tint, and takes its title from the peculiar character impressed upon it by the influence of the atmosphere—cracking it in divisions, like a Roman pavement. Remains of trees have been found in this bed, and markings of worms on the surface. This sandstone appears in many places—at the mouth of the Tikiria, and around Konia, continuing westward to Borupur. It re-appears at Dourisai, dipping westward, till a fault again cuts it off; and it is found once more at Porah, on the same river, whence it proceeds, with a westerly dip, till it becomes covered by shales to the west of Kerjang; re-appearing in the valley near Balhan, in Rehrakōl. In no place does this bed exceed two hundred feet in thickness.

The nodular shales have been estimated at nearly double this; they are blue, dove-coloured, and slightly green, fine in texture, and sometimes appear with beds of sand. In the neighbourhood of the Brahmini they occasionally almost disappear in the sandstone beneath, while their upper surface has received layers of a different character to its proper deposits. These shales are indicated by fragments of the same material on the soil, and by the thinness of the jungle growing above them. They rest on the lower sandstone, near Bijgole, and to the west of Dering, in the Tikiria Nullah, about two miles to the west of Kerjang Hill Station. Constant faults occurring in the strata, interrupt them, but their course can be traced without much difficulty.

The carboniferous series are in three divisions: the lower is described by Messrs. Blanford and Theobald, as shales and coarse sandstone interstratified, particularly at the base, the carboniferous shales of Talcheer, Gopalprosad, and those in another place, and interstratifications of blue and black shale, often very micaceous, with iron-stone, and coarse felspathic sandstone. These beds are fossiliferous, and are the sources of the coal and iron of the district. They contain remains of an ancient flora, chiefly vertebraria—*pecopteris*, *glossopteris*, and *trezygia*—and extend for nearly thirty miles, from the banks of the Brahmini to beyond the village of Antigura, and also to the vicinity of Patrapara.

Many of the shales contain seams of coal, varying in thickness from three inches to six feet, and are highly carbonaceous. At Patrapara, owing to an abundance of iron pyrites, spontaneous combustion has occurred, and jungle fires in other places have led to some of the beds being ignited.

The upper grit series at Mahadewa are quartzose and coarse sandstone, and conglomerates—the latter predominating near the bottom. Extensive denudation has taken place, particularly to the west of their area of deposit, showing how great has been the action of water upon them; while the appearance of bands of pebbles, one near Jutosora, near Rehrakōl, indicate an ancient beach. They form the Ghora Hills, the Konjire Hill, and other small elevations, cover one half of the coal-field, and rise into ridges of great height, sometimes up to one thousand five hundred feet.

An alluvium of sand and gravel, frequently ferruginous, occurs in many places, spreading over a vast area, sometimes to a considerable depth; in the Ouli valley it exceeds a hundred feet in thickness. On the Brahmini, the lower portion passes into laterite—a porous ferruginous rock, of concretionary structure—which occurs, to some extent, round Cuttack, and on the hills between there and Balasore, besides appearing in small patches on the plains. West of Talcheer it thickens considerably, and forms hills between Baypūr and Rasul, on the Cuttack and Ungool road, of from a hundred and fifty to two hundred feet above the level of the sea. It is produced by the infiltration of ferruginous matter—peroxide of iron—in the springs, which changes the character of the material on which it acts, whether it be a white clay, as in the neighbourhood of Midnapore, or among a bed of pebbles, as at the north of Cuttack, which it has cemented into a conglomerate. At Kinkerai, on the borders of Talcheer and Ungool, fragments of coarse sandstone, forming the bed of a nullah, have been impregnated with peroxide of iron, to the extent of sixty-six per cent.

Kunkur, too, appears in the alluvium, and penetrates the porous beds of the grits. This is produced by water containing carbonate of lime. A much harder rock, quartz, forms hills of considerable elevation. Bodaberna and Kerjang are chiefly composed of it. Quartz pebbles, too, are abundant. They suggest an extensive formation, coeval with the other primary rocks, the bulk of which has perished by disintegration. The gold that is said to have been found in the Tikiria, the Ouli, and Brahmini rivers, in all probability was washed out of the original quartz matrix at some very remote period. The Ouli flows through a sandstone district, but the extent of the changes the country has undergone will permit of the metal having originally belonged to an earlier rock.

Although the frequent occurrence of faults denotes considerable disturbance, the only evidence of volcanic action is to be found in the intrusion of igneous into metamorphic rocks. More than one change of level has no doubt taken place, but as yet the survey has not been sufficiently minute or comprehensive to afford data for a reliable opinion as to what amount of change has been produced by marine or fluvial denudation, and what by gradual elevation and depression.

Taking a commercial view of the geological features I have described, it is impossible to deny that elements of prosperity exist in the building stones, and in the iron ores; and, notwithstanding the unsatisfactory reports of the coal fields, I do not doubt that under favourable circumstances they will be worked to a profit. At present the want of proper facilities for transport would be fatal to any enterprise to develope these resources; but when the jungle has been cleared, and available roads completed, the principal obstacle to the profitable working of the coal measures will have been removed.

With regard to the building materials in Orissa, the stone in most request is laterite, which has been largely employed for walls, as well as for structures of importance. "Few rocks," says an able geologist, "present greater advantages from its peculiar character; it is easy to cut and shape when first dug, and it becomes hard and tough after exposure to the air, while it seems to be very little acted on by the weather. Indeed, in many of the sculptured stones of some of the oldest buildings, temples, &c., in the district, the chisel marks are as fresh and sharp as when [the edifice was] first built. It is perhaps not so strong, nor so capable of resisting great pressure, or bearing great weights, as some of the sandstones, or the more compact kinds of gneiss; but it certainly possesses amply sufficient strength for all ordinary purposes. It is largely used at the present time; but has also been employed from the earliest period from which the temples and buildings of the country date; and the elaborate specimens of carving and ornament which some of them present, show that the nodular structure and irregular surface of the laterite does not prevent its effective use for such purposes of ordinary ornamentation as mouldings, &c."*

We are assured by the same authority, that slabs, from four to five feet in length, are easily procurable of this useful stone. These are quarried by splitting, after grooves have been made with a pick. The gravelly laterite makes excellent road material. A more detailed account of it has been added by Mr. W. T. Blanford, who divides it into surface laterite found in ferruginous nodules of from an eighth to a quarter of an inch in diameter, in a matrix of dark reddish brown clay, more or less sandy; and black laterite, forming solid masses, covering a considerable area, which often passes into gravel.

It is probable that both are the remains of a metamorphic rock, which has suffered materially by denudation, and that the disintegrated portions have been transported from their proper base, in the shape of nodules, pebbles, and gravel, and reconsolidated into masses. This appears to have been rendered sufficiently clear by the section of a well dug at Daltolah, near Khurdah, under the direction of Captain Harris, surveyor of the Cuttack rivers, the first six feet of which was through the nodular and sandy de-

* "On the Geological Structure and Physical Features of the Districts of Bancoorah, Midnapore, and Orissa."—"Geological Survey of India," i., 249.

posit; then came the argillaceous form of laterite, varying in colour from dark red, reddish brown, dark yellowish brown, and light yellow, till at twenty-five feet it became all yellow or white; while the boring below showed a gradual passage into gneiss. At Paikesae, a village to the west of the river Dyah, blocks of gneiss may be observed, surrounded by laterite. A ferruginous clay, derived from a felspathic rock, is often found underlying it, and is called lithomarge; and the iron this contains is apparently derived by percolation through the upper bed. But the source of the metal in the latter has not as yet been established. Mr. Blanford has suggested that it is produced by the magnetic iron—a component part of the metamorphic rock—having been converted by the action of oxygen and water into the hydrated peroxide of the laterite. Be this as it may, the presence of the metal adds considerably to the value of the stone. An analysis of the laterite found at Daltola gave 24·5 per cent. of iron.

Lieutenant Rigby, an engineer officer employed in the province of Cuttack, devoted his attention to the building materials furnished by the district in stone and timber. Of the former he describes several kinds —one known to the people by the name of Koudah, which he found at Killah Mootree, on the river Mahanuddy, about ten miles above Cuttack. It is employed mostly for cornices and screen work in the native buildings. With rude tools it is cut from the hills by a slow process, at a cost of about three and a half annas per yard of three cubic feet—its carriage to Cuttack costing nearly half as much more.

The second is the laterite already described, which he found abundant, and in common use. This is employed for the same purpose as the first—is brought from the Chutteal hills, is one-seventh dearer, and its carriage costs six annas per yard, which makes it too expensive for ordinary purposes. This is called Bolemallah. There is another stone, known as Moogney, that has been used in the Black Pagoda for the sculptured figures there. It is very expensive, as it costs in the bazaars twelve rupees a yard; and is said to be brought from a considerable distance southward.

There are also two kinds of lime in use, one produced from shells collected on the coast about Manickpatum; the other from kunker, brought principally from Dehnuddee.

Iron, he adds, is procurable in the bazaar to almost any extent, the principal portion of the ore coming from the river Mahanuddy, about a hundred and fifty miles above Cuttack. But the timber floated down the river in rafts from the forests, by his account, is both large in quantity and various in quality. He enumerates twelve different kinds, all of which are valuable either for building, or for domestic furniture.*

Gneiss is a valuable stone both to the builder and the sculptor; in India many of the Hindoo temples and idols are carved in it. Such are the statues in the Black Pagoda at Canarue, near Pooree; millstones and drinking-cups are also shaped out of it. It might be worked to a very large extent. Sandstone, too, can be quarried extensively, as it has been at an early period of Orissan history. Evidence of this may be seen in the temples of Bohanessur and in the caves of Khundegeree.

The chloritic rock and serpentine are also available for any purpose to which they can be turned; a large supply in blocks of any size is easily procurable. At present these valuable materials are little used, except when rudely fashioned into plates, bowls, basins, and other domestic utensils, to be sold in the different villages.

The laterite differs only in the presence of iron from kaolin, but an excellent material for porcelain may be found in the soft white clay used by the people for dressing leather, and as a wash for whitening their dwellings. This abounds in the sandstone,

* Journal of the Asiatic Society of Bengal for 1842, p. 836.

while several of the alluvial clays may be burnt into good bricks.

Among the natural products of the country the most profitable is salt, which more than half a century ago, when a monopoly, realised an annual revenue of nearly eighteen lacs of rupees, or £180,000 sterling. In the old process it was manufactured from sea water, thickened with the brine which dries on the shore after high tides. This was boiled to evaporation, in oblong earthen pots, and the salt, as it was produced, taken with iron ladles, and formed into heaps, which were protected from the weather by a covering of reeds. The whitest and purest, styled Pangah, used to be greatly esteemed in India, and the manufacturers had a considerable and profitable trade.

Another staple is rice, which is cultivated extensively, and the surplus, after supplying the home demand, is forwarded to the native merchants at Calcutta, for consumption in India, or export. It used to be, north of the Byterini, almost the only grain raised; but it was large and coarse—inferior in quality to the best Bengal crops. There were several kinds raised in different districts, and at different periods of the year.

Much of the soil is poor, both in the hills and plains, which is easily accounted for by the nature of the formation; for where the gneiss is not evident the surface is a dry sand, on a gravel mixed with limestone concretions, or a tenacious clay, where there is no vegetation but brushwood and rank grass. In the thick jungle, grows the fragrant *Pandanus Odoratissimus*, from the flowers of which a distilled water is made, as well as a medicinal stimulant; and the obstacles to progress are much increased by the presence of different species of Euphorbia and Mimosa. Groves of Mango and of Banyan, here and there, afford a pleasant shade from the heat, though not a secure one, for wild beasts and poisonous reptiles are often concealed there, and a still more fatal enemy lurks about in the shape of miasma—an attack from which the European seldom escapes.

Dr. Hooker, in his "Flora Indica," has illustrated the botany of Orissa, but from his description it does not appear that his explorations extended to this obscure portion of India. The botany of the coast and forests had been previously investigated by Roxburgh, who resided for a considerable period at Samulcottah, in what are still called the Northern Circars; the result of his researches appeared in his "Flora Indica," and in the extensive collections he made in that territory. Dr. Russell also procured a large number of plants from the same locality.

The characteristics of the flora of the country are thus described:—

"The forests which cover the slopes of the outer ranges are very dense, and though not equal in luxuriance or variety to those of Malabar and Malaya, they are richer in ferns than those of Mysore; many Malabar plants, not found in the Carnatic, or in the Eastern Ghats, recurring in these more northern jungles. Thus the wild pepper is found there abundantly, with numerous Zinziberacæ, and orchids, Arengu Saccharifera, and, perhaps, Caryota, but apparently no other palm. Species of Dillenia, Leca, Mimusops, Bassia, Roxburghia, &c., also occur. The forests which cover the mountains of the interior are much drier, and are separated by open valleys, more or less under cultivation." *

Among the oil-producing plants must be noticed the Sursoon *(Sinapis ramosa)*. Rape *(Sinapis dichotoma)* bears the same Indian name, and they are often cultivated together. The stalks are used as fodder; cattle also are fed on the cake made from the pressed seed; but the oil from the mustard seed is taken in the way of butter by the natives, particularly in their curries. A thinner and purer oil is extracted from Til *(Sesanum Orientale)*, but it is used exclusively for

* Introductory Essay to the "Flora Indica." By J. D. Hooker, M.D. R.N., F.R.S., and Thomas Thomson, M.D., F.L.S.

perfumery, and to flavour sweetmeats; the cake, however, is accepted as food both by man and beast. The safflower produces an abundant crop of seed, from which an oil is extracted that burns brilliantly. But the castor-oil plant is more generally cultivated, partly perhaps because it grows in the cleared jungle with very little labour, and partly because there is always and everywhere a lively demand for the produce. When extracted by the native process, it is used for lubricating leather and for burning in lamps; but in European hands it becomes a much more valuable commodity.

The poppy can be raised in almost any of the cleared districts, not only for the extract so well known as opium, but for the seeds, which are innoxious, and are eaten freely. So is the cake, when the oil has been expressed, which is not only limpid, but wholesome; and though an objection has been raised against it for burning rapidly, it has been recommended as an addition to the kitchen for all purposes for which olive oil is now employed.

There is a large tree called Mahawah *(Bassia Latifolia)*, from the flower buds of which a distilled water is made, of great fragrance; while, when pressed into cake, they are as much relished by the natives as by their cattle. A kernel containing two or three seeds remains after the blossom has dropped; from this a kind of half liquid butter is produced, of which, as well as of the residue, the people are particularly fond; and the forest trees, such as the Murb *(Melia Azuderachto)*, and Chironjee *(Chironja Sapida)*, produce a sweetish fruit and kernel, which, when dried, is a favourite Indian delicacy.

Foreign varieties of the sugar-cane have been introduced into the province with considerable success; but the red Bombay cane is the one in common cultivation. The improved culture, and the better variety, insures a much larger crop; but sugar might be obtained from this portion of India in greatly increased quantities. When planted in the garden at Cuttack, the stalks grew, in 1844, to a height of eight feet, and were very thick. A great number of fruit trees, flowers, and vegetables have been successfully raised on the same ground, according to a report from Captain W. W. Dunlop, secretary of the Branch Agri-Horticultural Society, published in the Journal of the Agricultural and Horticultural Society of India for that year.

Tobacco of excellent quality has also been introduced by the same channel; and having been experimentally grown at Cuttack, has been distributed through the district, like the sugar-cane. Attempts have been made to cultivate latakia, and other choice species of this valuable plant, in India. Cuttack has now its annual shows of fruit, flowers, and vegetables, when prizes are given for the best competitors. Its garden is a branch establishment of the Agricultural and Horticultural Society of India.

A better system of cultivation might easily be introduced into the hill estates, much jungle cleared, and the slopes of the smaller elevations prepared for crops of indigo, rice, cotton, and poppy; in short, for anything for which the soil and climate are adapted. The landholders and husbandmen of Goomsur have too long been content with exchanging ginger, turmeric, yams, mustard, and other easily raised produce, for bullocks, and cotton cloth, salt, and fish brought by the travelling dealers; or of con veying them for barter to such marts as Sooradah and Ballaguntah. A kind of fair is held at Gaddapur, Kalahundy, and Porala, near Russelcondah, where the native merchants bring silk and cotton fabrics, ploughs, and domestic utensils, beads, and other personal decorations, articles of food, and iron, brass, and copper vessels.

The sugar-cane has been raised at Sarangaddah to a slight extent, and the produce disposed of at Ballaguntah, to be distributed in Boad and Goomsur; and when good roads render the traffic easy, there would be no difficulty in establishing the cultivation on a large scale.

Of live stock there is neither abundance nor variety; nor can either cattle or sheep be recommended for their breed. Bullocks and buffaloes are used as beasts of burthen, and yoked for the plough. Milch cows are few. The sheep are small, but the mutton is excellent. Goats are abundant, and so are pigs; but the latter is scarcely an improvement on the jungle swine. The Khond also raises poultry, especially pea-fowl.

His agricultural instruments comprise a light plough, that does little more than scarify the soil; a harrow, having wooden teeth in a double row; a sickle, an axe, and a wood-cutting knife.

The fauna of this part of Hindostan includes an animal called, in Orissa, Bujjer Kapta *(Manis Crassicandata)*, about three feet six inches long, and is a very rare quadruped in India. It lives in the fissures of rocks, among the jungles, feeding principally upon the large black ant, which its long tongue enables it to secure easily. It is slow in motion, awkward and heavy in appearance, and when disturbed rolls itself into a ball, with its nose buried under its belly, and its tail surrounding its body like a wrapper. When uncoiled, the upper portion appears to be clothed in a kind of clay-coloured scale armour, terminating in a broad scaly tail, on which it can rest, supported by the hind feet only. These scales the Hindoos consider to possess peculiar medicinal properties for the cure of hæmorrhoides. The undefended portion of the manis is of a pale brownish-white.

Specimens of this quadruped may be seen in the collection of natural history in the British Museum, and a detailed description of one, with illustrations, is given by Lieutenant R. S. Tickell, in the Journal of the Asiatic Society of Bengal.*

Off the coast, fish are abundant, and in considerable variety. The most prized are members of the *Pleuronectidæ*, such as soles, pomfret; *Merlangus vulgaris*, whiting; some of the *Mugilidæ*, the mullet; and a great number, better known by their Indian names. There is also plenty of crustaceans, molluscs, and turtle. Fresh-water fish abound in the rivers, as angling is not followed by the natives. The fishermen who carry on their occupation at sea use only nets suspended on tall bamboo poles, with which, at the flood tide, particularly on the northern coast, they take large hawls. As many as sixty-one different kinds of fish, all excellent as food, are known to the fishermen. They are conveyed to the nearest villages, where they find a ready market.

* For the year 1842, p. 221.

APPENDIX.

APPENDIX.

Extract from a Letter from the Secretary to the Government of India, to Lieutenant-Colonel J. Campbell, C.B., Agent in the Hill Tracts of Orissa, dated 12*th February*, 1849, *with reference to the Campaign against Ungool.*

I am directed to inform you that the Right Honourable the Governor-General in Council* considers that you have conducted the duty with which you were charged in a manner highly satisfactory; and His Lordship in Council desires me to convey to you the thanks of the Government for the promptitude and decision with which this service has been performed.

* Lord Hardinge.

Extract from a Letter from Secretary to the Government of India, with the Governor-Genernl, dated 28th April, 1849.

In reply, I am directed to observe that the Governor-General* considers this Report as a very sensible and most satisfactory one, and to request that you will convey to Lieutenant-Colonel Campbell the Governor-General's approbation of the firmness, skill, and judgment which he has displayed in the performance of the arduous duties committed to him, and to assure him of the lively satisfaction which His Lordship has experienced in learning the full and happy results of his exertions.

From F. J. Halliday, Esq., Secretary to the Government of India, to Lieutenant-Colonel J. Campbell, C.B., Agent in the Hill Tracts of Orissa, dated 16th June, 1849.

SIR,

I am directed to acknowledge the receipt of your letter, dated the 31st ultimo, with its enclosure, and in reply to assure you of the great regret with which the President † in Council has learnt that the state of

* Lord Dalhousie. † Sir Herbert Maddock.

your health compels you to resign your appointment. During the period you have been at the head of the Agency for the Suppression of the Meriah sacrifice, the Government have had every reason to be satisfied with the progress which has been made towards the extinction of that rite, and equally so with the commencement which you have made in the adoption of measures for the suppression of the crime of female infanticide. Your proceedings have always appeared to be judicious, and well adapted for effecting the great end in view, and from your continuance at the head of the Agency, the Government had confidently anticipated the early and complete extirpation of the Meriah rite within the limits of the tract of country under your supervision.

From George Couper, Esq., Under-Secretary to the Government of India, dated 3rd March, 1851.

Sir,

I am directed to acknowledge the receipt of Colonel Campbell's letter, dated the 9th ultimo, and in reply to convey the expression of the satisfaction of the Governor-General in Council, at the results, as therein reported, of the operations of the Orissa Agency during the past season.

From F. F. Courtenay, Esq., Private Secretary to the Most Noble the Governor-General of India, to Major-General Campbell, C.B., dated 11*th April*, 1855.

Lord Dalhousie desires me to express to you his regret at learning that the state of your health is such as to cause the loss to the Government of India of services which he has frequently had occasion to appreciate so highly, and approve so cordially, as those which you have rendered in the Hill Tracts of Orissa.

The following observations are extracted from a despatch from the Honourable the Court of Directors, dated 14th June, 1854, and were forwarded to the Head-Quarters of the Agency, after my departure, by the Secretary to the Government of India, who stated that the Governor-General, Lord Dalhousie, felt assured that the Agency would receive with satisfaction this approving testimony, emanating from the highest authority.

"In conducting the operations, and dealing with

the rude inhabitants of the country, the officers of the Agency have experienced no ordinary difficulties, and appear to have shown a wise discretion and a clear perception of the best method to secure success. They have maintained an attitude of firmness, without unnecessary resort to forcible measures. They have calmed angry feelings by conciliation, and have opposed rational persuasion to popular prejudice and error. They have substituted confidence by temperate explanation in personal conferences. The means of conciliation have been so well directed in the majority of instances, as not only to overcome the opposition, but to obtain the co-operation of the leading men.

"Viewing the Meriah operations as a whole, they have been highly successful, and are creditable to the officers concerned; nor is it in measures of repression alone that we see cause for present satisfaction and future hope.

"It is obvious that the germs of an ultimate civilization have been planted in the country, and we may entertain a confident hope that the advance of the population towards a higher social condition will be in an accelerated ratio of progress."

HUMAN SACRIFICES IN ORISSA.

Extracted from "Friend of India," dated September 28th, 1854.

All over India the warfare against the darker crimes is everywhere proceeding, and everywhere successful. Mr. Gubbins at Agra, Mr. Montgomery in the Punjab, and Mr. C. Raikes everywhere, are weaning the people from their habit of infanticide. Though thuggee by poisoning still flourishes, thuggee in its traditional form may be considered almost extinct. Captain Hervey at Bombay pursues the criminal tribes who wander over the Western Presidency. Mr. Jackson in Bengal is enlarging the sphere of his operations against the Dacoits, and his hands will speedily be strengthened. Finally, Colonel Campbell reports from Orissa the almost entire suppression of the practice of offering human victims, once as prevalent in Khondistan as in Carthage. In every one of these cases it must be remembered that the crime has been attacked by a special agency, armed with exceptional powers, and backed by laws which recognise the principle that crime is deserving of punishment, and not of impunity.

Hitherto the difficulties in the way of the Government of India have been almost entirely moral. Thuggee as well as infanticide have flourished almost entirely through the deadness of the moral sense, and of the natural affections. They were not regarded as crimes by those who committed them, and, like drunkenness in England, required preventive even more than retributive legislation. In Bombay, the difficulty with the criminal races is the hereditary character of the tribes, who, like the gipsies in Europe, consider theft and fortune-telling as their natural occupations, the work they were born to do. Even in Bengal, the great cause of dacoity is the cowardice of the people, who are afraid either to cut down the dacoit, or to bear testimony against him. In Orissa, there were, in addition to these moral impediments to improvement, a physical one of no small magnitude. The Khonds are not only dead to all sense of their crime, and confident that it is directly sanctioned by the deity, but they also dwell in fastnesses which it is scarcely possible to invade. The moral obliquity which protects the Whiteboy in Ireland, and the physical circumstances which guard the banditti in Calabria, are here united, and in their most impracticable form. Legislation is useless among a people without the pale of law. Threats are absurd where they cannot be enforced even by a campaign. Bribery is powerless when the people believe a crime to be their greatest earthly gain, and moral suasion seems impracticable when applied to races who would consider a Missionary an acceptable offering to the Gods. The British Government, if placed in such circumstances, would probably employ force, as it has done on the coast of Africa; or let crime and people perish together, as in some parts of the continent of Australia. The Indian Government has not adopted either course. It has neither shut its eyes to a fearful crime, nor attempted to bring wild tribes back to humanity by wholesale slaughter. A succession of Agents, trained in the school of Indian Politicals, have, for twenty-five years, steadily brought the moral influence, derived from irresistible physical strength, to bear upon the crime.

We have no intention of passing again over ground already familiar to our readers. Still less are we about to re-open the controversy as to which of three able officers may have obtained the greatest measure of personal success. We confine ourselves strictly to an analysis of the measures adopted for the suppression of the crime, and the degree of success that has been attained. The infected district stretches down the coast from the borders of the Orissa mountains far into Madras, over a territory as large as Wales. The country, itself semi-independent, forms part of two Presidencies, and it was not till 1845 that the Government centralized their operations by the creation of a separate agency.

From that moment the practice of human offerings rapidly declined. Every clan obeys its own chief, and every chief found it advantageous not to be at war with the great Empire beyond his borders. Here was at once a ground of influence. Every chief was informed that his favour from the British Government depended entirely upon his efforts for the suppression of human offerings. The majority consented, but their promises were broken, and the people, who are convinced their temporal welfare depends upon the practice, were as indignant as Tetzel when his indulgences were denounced. In some districts they became turbulent. Their chiefs were protected from their wrath, their country was opened by rough jungle paths, and they themselves were overawed by bodies of troops traversing their most inaccessible jungles. In other districts, numbers of children purchased for slaughter are intended to labour as slaves, and the purchasers fancied they would lose money while incurring vengeance from above. Their fears were quieted, and as soon as sound guarantees were obtained for the victims' lives, the boys were left to labour. In some places, again, young women were retained by the chiefs as concubines, and afterwards sacrificed to the gods. The chiefs were persuaded to marry them, and thus put an end to all danger of their lives.

All victims preparing for sacrifice were demanded, and usually conceded, and, during 1852-53, in only one instance was it necessary to employ the *ultima ratio* of force. Even in this case Colonel Campbell was attacked before he permitted his men to fire, and this solitary act of severity has produced the best effects. The determination of the Government, maintained for half a generation, the incessant visits to the hills, and the surveillance which, amid a passive or discontented population, is almost marvellous, have convinced the mountaineers that resistance is impossible. Right or wrong, with their creed, or against their creed, the practice must be abandoned. It is abandoned accordingly. In Boad, where the slaughter of children was carried to an extent we are almost afraid to record—where bits of flesh, cut from living men, were strewed on the field as a miraculous manure—where the land, so to speak, was guanoed with human blood, the practice has ceased to exist. In the Chinna Kimedy mountains it is also suppressed, and Colonel Campbell thus records the existing sentiment of the people :—

"Each chief was invited freely to express his sentiment on this important subject, which many did without hesitation, saying, that when we first came among them they were like beasts in the jungle, doing as their fathers had done before them; they now clearly comprehended that our only object in coming was to stop human sacrifice; not a fowl, or anything else, was taken, not even a fence was injured by the people of the camp; their fields produced crops as good as formerly, and sickness was not more prevalent; it was no use resisting the orders of the Sircar; their Meriahs had been all removed, moreover, they cost much money, and they were now of one mind, determined never more to have anything to do with human sacrifice. In two or three places it was asked, 'What shall we say to the deity?' They were told to say whatever they pleased, when the spokesman repeated the following formula: 'Do not be angry with us, O Goddess! for giving you the blood of beasts instead of human blood, but vent your wrath upon that gentleman, who is well able to bear it; we are guiltless.'"

Nor is that all. The very source of the crime has been attacked. The people have become convinced that famine does not follow the abolition of the practice. They have been relieved of a severe money pressure, caused by the purchase of the victims. They are entering more and more into the commerce of the plains, and are cultivating every year a wider breadth of ground. Finally, we would fain believe that, degraded as these tribes have been, the natural instinct which forbids the shedding of unnecessary blood, and the natural affection which makes men guard their young, are recovering their force. In eighteen years a crime worse than any known in Europe has been eradicated—twelve hundred and sixty human beings have been preserved from a horrible death—an entire people has been induced to forego a crime sanctioned alike by antiquity and by superstition—and a district as large as Wales has been raised a whole grade in the career of civilization. All this has been effected by a Government declared to be oppressive, and by the class whom India honours, and England stigmatizes as Politicals.

We have but one word to add. Colonel Campbell has been concerned in these operations from the first. His firm gentleness has made them successful in the end. He has spent no small portion of a life away from civilization, and in a scene where his efforts have been honoured only by philanthropists. Had he destroyed in battle the number he has saved from immolation, he would have received honours which should not be denied only because of his modest appreciation of his own success.

THE ILLUSTRATIONS.

THE engravings with which this work is illustrated, being generally sufficiently clear, in the light of the preceding narrative, to tell their own story, any further allusion to them might be deemed unnecessary. As they are all, however, intended to represent real scenes in the country of the Khonds, and actual events in the history of the natives, a few additional words of explanation may be considered neither superfluous nor uninteresting.

HUMAN SACRIFICE AS PRACTISED IN GOOMSUR.

There are various forms of Meriah sacrifice in use among the different Khond tribes, some of which have been described in the text. The Frontispiece is simply an attempt, and a somewhat imperfect one, to give the reader an idea of one of the forms, perhaps the simplest and least cruel, in which human sacrifice, as stated by eye-witnesses, is performed in parts of Upper Goomsur. The victim, being brought to the place selected in the forest, is fastened to a post, and after some invocations by the officiating priest, cut to pieces by the excited Khonds, each of whom, appropriating a morsel of the bloody flesh, hastens to bury it in his field, thereby, as he believes, presenting an acceptable offering to the Earth Goddess. It is superfluous to add that no European ever saw a sacrifice offered.

RESCUED MERIAH WOMAN AND CHILDREN.

The subject of the Vignette is a woman named Hoolloo Mai, who, with her children, had long dwelt in safety at Bundhasir of Kalahundy, when the Khonds of that district having determined to offer up a human sacrifice, this poor creature was selected. The Tat Rajah of Tooamool, who had long been won over to our views, hearing of the intention of his Khonds, and having in vain endeavoured to dissuade them from their bloody purpose, wrote a hasty note on dried palm leaves to the British Agent, stating the imminence of the sacrifice, and his own unsuccessful efforts to prevent it. No time was lost, and a trusty man was despatched in haste with a small body of irregular troops to save the victim. After a rapid march of twenty-two hours, this party reached the appointed place just as the mournful ceremony was commencing. The woman, Hoolloo Mai, very heavily ironed, was being carried round the village of Pucknagoodah in solemn procession, escorted by music and multitudes of Khonds. At this critical moment a scene of intense dramatic interest occurred; the armed party of the British Government, led by a worthy chief, named Bhag Singhi, broke through the crowd, arrested the procession, and demanded the victim; the exasperated and excited Khonds brandished their battle axes, and refused to yield the trembling woman, already half dead with fright, and so heavily manacled that she could not stir. Bhag Singhi acted with the resolution demanded by the occasion; he seized the cot on which the woman was carried, surrounded it with armed men, ranged his small band in battle array, and fought his way gallantly back to the Agent's camp, bringing Hoolloo Mai in triumph with him. Although there was great excitement, and some firing, no lives were lost. When this poor woman made known that she had left two children, who might share the fate intended for her, no time was lost in adopting the necessary measures for their rescue, and both mother and children are now living happily in one of our Meriah villages near Russelcondah. Hoolloo Mai has quite regained her health and strength. The warrior, Bagh Singhi, who behaved so well on this trying occasion, had a very handsome armlet presented to him, by order of the Supreme Government of India, in recognition of his gallant achievement. This man was one of the oldest and most valued of my little body of irregular soldiers.

OORYAH CHIEF.

The engraving at page 16 represents an Ooryah Chief of Khondistan, with Khond weapons in the background. This will give the reader a good idea of the difference between the pure Khond Chief and the Ooryah or Hindoo Chief of the Khonds. The relations in which they stand to each other is fully described in my narrative. This chief is dressed out as on festival occasions. The battle axes in the background are the different kinds used by the Khonds.

SEBUNDIES AT RUSSELCONDAH PREPARING FOR THEIR DEPARTURE TO THE KHOND HILLS.

This sketch (p. 65) represents a few of my native irregular soldiers on the plain at Russelcondah, preparing for their departure to the Khond hills, distant about twelve miles. The barracks of these troops were at Russelcondah, where they generally remained during the monsoon, or rainy season.

KHOND CHIEFS OF CHINNA KIMEDY IN THEIR ORDINARY COSTUME.

The engraving at page 120 represents two chiefs, or mullikos, of Chinna Kimedy. The one on the right is named Gongho Mulliko, the other Dollah Mulliko. They both took part in the Khond councils, without displaying any particular intelligence, but they are good average specimens of the pure Khond chiefs. Nothing can be more primitive than the costume in which they are presented, which is that worn by them on ordinary occasions.

RESCUED MERIAH VICTIMS.

The plates at pages 132 and 213 represent two distinct groups of rescued Meriah victims, male and female, who have long resided in our Meriah villages mentioned in the narrative. The four girls in the second engraving, all of whom are in the daily village dress of the female inhabitants of the plains, are the wives of the four youths in the preceding illustration, who are all represented in their ordinary village dress. The fifth youth, named Dengah, was rescued from the Boad country, and as he retains a predilection for his old hill costume, he was photographed in full dress, a distinction of which he is not a little proud.

THE END.

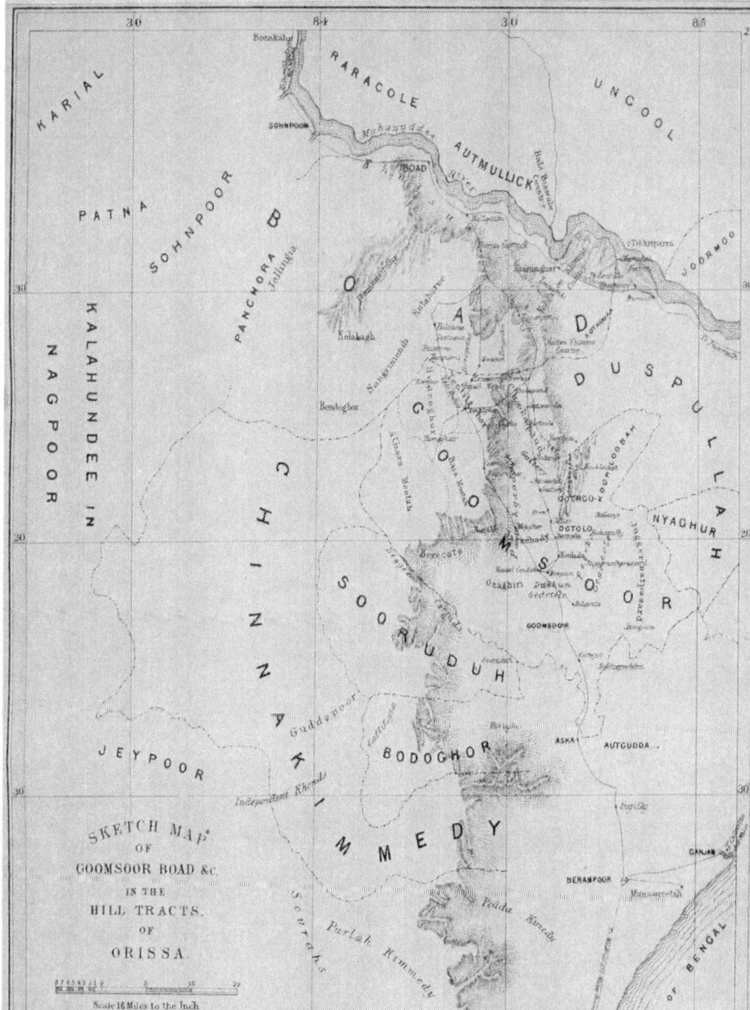

London, Hurst & Blackett, Great Marlborough Street, 1864.